FIFTY YEARS IN
Dyslexia Research

FIFTY YEARS IN
Dyslexia Research

by
T.R. MILES

John Wiley & Sons, Ltd

Chichester · New York · Weinheim · Brisbane · Toronto · Singapore

Other Wiley Editorial Offices

John Wiley & Sons Inc., 111 River Street, Hoboken, NJ 07030, USA

Jossey-Bass, 989 Market Street, San Francisco, CA 94103-1741, USA

Wiley-VCH Verlag GmbH, Boschstr. 12, D-69469 Weinheim, Germany

John Wiley & Sons Australia Ltd, 42 McDougall Street, Milton, Queensland 4064, Australia

John Wiley & Sons (Asia) Pte Ltd, 2 Clementi Loop #02-01, Jin Xing Distripark, Singapore 129809

John Wiley & Sons Canada Ltd, 22 Worcester Road, Etobicoke, Ontario, Canada M9W 1L1

Wiley also publishes its books in a variety of electronic formats. Some content that appears in print may not be available in electronic books.

Library of Congress Cataloging-in-Publication Data

Miles, T. R. (Thomas Richard)
Fifty years in dyslexia research / by T.R. Miles.
   p. ; cm.
   Includes bibliographical references and index.
   ISBN-13: 978-0-470-02747-9 (cloth : alk. paper)
   ISBN-10: 0-470-02747-9 (cloth : alk. paper)
   1. Dyslexia. 2. Dyslexia–History. I. Title.
   [DNLM: 1. Dyslexia–history. 2. Dyslexia–classification.
   3. Dyslexia–diagnosis. 4. History, 20th Century. WL 340.6 M643f 2006]
RC394.W6M56 2006
616.85'53–dc22   2006011411

British Library Cataloguing in Publication Data

A catalogue record for this book is available from the British Library

ISBN -13 978-0-470-02747-9
ISBN -10 0-470-02747-9

Typeset in 10/12 pt Times Roman by Thomson Press (India) Limited, New Delhi, India.
Printed and bound in Great Britain by TJ International Ltd., Padstow, Cornwall.
This book is printed on acid-free paper responsibly manufactured from sustainable forestry in which at least two trees are planted for each one used for paper production.

Contents

Foreword

In this fascinating autobiographical account, Tim Miles leads us through the history of his involvement in the field of dyslexia and in so doing completes an important part of the jigsaw of the history of dyslexia in Britain. Tim Miles is well known as a pioneer of dyslexia, and most would characterise his scholarship as straddling psychological and philosophical inquiry. Here we learn that Tim's inspiration came from the careful study of individual cases; what unfolds is the development of an insightful theory of dyslexia that explains both empirical findings and clinical observations.

The thesis expounded in this book is that dyslexia is a syndrome – it is not the same as poor reading but a disorder that encompasses a range of symptoms that include problems of verbal labelling, arithmetic difficulties, verbal short-term-memory problems and subtle speech-production difficulties. Miles is not reductionist; he has long believed that all of these signs provide clues as to the nature of dyslexia and he has been at pains to operationalise the definitioin of dyslexia through his widely known 'Bangor Dyslexia Test'. Not satisfied with quantifying the syndrome in this way, he has tested his theory with reference to epidemiological data in the British Births Cohort Study, and it has stood up well. With his wife Elaine and colleagues in Bangor he has closed a virtuous circle, wherein theory has motivated teaching and diagnostic assessments of children and adults, and practical work has guided theory.

In parallel with theoretical developments in the field of dyslexia, Miles also witnessed changes in the views of the educational establishment with respect to children with specific reading difficulties. His initial cases were patients referred to Child Guidance clinics, and the predominant view was that these children had emotional problems. But Miles was perplexed that psychodynamic theories could not account for the consistent patterns of 'reversals', subtle language difficulties, problems of musical notation and extraordinary spelling problems that these children experienced. Rather, he thought that the problem was constitutional in origin, likely to be some form of developmental aphasia. But the world of education was not ready to accept this view and battles raged as to whether 'dyslexia' should be considered a medical or an educational issue. Key landmarks in the struggle for recognition included Miles' involvement in the establishment of the Word-Blind Centre in London in the 1960s, the inauguration of the British Dyslexia Association in 1972 and the establishment of the Dyslexia Unit in Bangor, which was to offer teaching to children in schools in north Wales in an important early partnership with the local education authority long before such alliances were the norm. There was also much going on behind the scenes; the establishment of the first Master's degree in dyslexia at Bangor, to elevate the skills of practitioners of dyslexia, and meetings of proponents of the different teaching methods used in the UK which confirmed that, for teaching people with dyslexia, the preferred teaching strategy was structured, cumulative, multisensory teaching.

This compelling and accessible account takes us on an intriguing journey that follows the curiosity of one of the pioneers of dyslexia through fifty years of scholarship. It does not shy away from difficult issues such as the role of IQ in the assessment of dyslexia, whether or not there are subtypes and whether dyscalculia should be considered a separate syndrome from dyslexia. Miles' work presages much contemporary neuroscientific research on dyslexia. Importantly, current knowledge confirms that his clinical intuitions were right: dyslexia does have a genetic basis and is characterised by atypical brain function. It can be characterised as a syndrome in that a core phonological deficit can explain a wide range of the signs and symptoms that are experienced by people with dyslexia, beyond reading and spelling. Moreover, there are also what Miles calls 'dyslexia variants' – people who show some but not all of the signs and whose difficulties may not be sufficient to fully qualify for the label. Thus, in families of parents with dyslexia, offspring may share dyslexic characteristics but not all succumb to reading problems (referred to as the broader phenotype of dyslexia). Finally, and most importantly, inheriting the risk of dyslexia need not be a cause for despair; early identification and appropriate teaching can do a great deal to ameliorate dyslexia and give those who are dyslexic the opportunity to use their talents to the full.

Margaret J. Snowling
York
September 2005

Preface

In the present book, as in its predecessor (Miles, 1993a), I have tried to maintain scientific rigour without over-burdening the main text with statistical technicalities. These are available for anyone who wishes to consult them, in the form of end-of-chapter notes.

Since my intention was to describe my own involvement with dyslexia research, I have added at the end of some of the chapters some personal recollections. These mostly relate to my encounters with the many interesting individuals whom I met over the years, and my hope is that they will add to the book's interest.

I should like to thank Dr E. Simmons for providing me with the opportunity to teach Brenda and Michael and for giving me the crucial cue – 'a form of aphasia' – which started me off on my dyslexia research.

Detailed acknowledgements to individuals will be found in the main body of the book. I would like, however, in this preface to pay tribute to those friends and colleagues whose ideas on dyslexia played a major part in influencing my own thinking. In particular I would like to thank my former tutor and mentor, Professor Oliver Zangwill, with whom I discussed the cases of Brenda and Michael in some detail. He initially reassured me by saying that he considered the findings on these two cases to be 'genuine and important'. Oliver Zangwill supported me in my dyslexia research up to the time of his death in 1987.

My thanks are also due to Professor Nick Ellis, Professor Rod Nicolson, Dr Angela Fawcett, Dr Mary Haslum, Professor Uta Frith and Professor John Stein and Professor Margaret Hubicki. I have learned much from all of them and enjoyed many stimulating discussions with them. I am also grateful for the encouragement which I have recently received from my colleagues in the School of Psychology at Bangor, Professor Virginia Muller Gathercole and Dr Guillaume Thierry. I should also like to acknowledge my debt to my colleagues at the Dyslexia Unit (attached to the School of Psychology), and in particular to Ann Cooke, Marie Jones, Dorothy Gilroy and Elizabeth du Pre.

Not least, I should like to pay tribute to those many dyslexic individuals of all ages who have been willing to talk to me about their hopes, fears and aspirations.

I should like to thank Professor Margaret Snowling both for writing the foreword to this book and for her advice and help over the presentation of its contents.

Finally, I wish to convey a special thank-you to Elaine, my wife. No words can adequately do justice to my debt to her. Quite apart from the encouragement and support which she has given to me for over fifty years, she is co-author with me of several books and book chapters, including Miles and Miles (1983a) and Miles and

Miles (1999a); she is also co-editor of Miles and Miles (2004). It is a real bonus to be a member of a husband-and-wife team each having a different contribution to make to the study of dyslexia.

T.R.M.
Bangor
2006

Acknowledgements

I am grateful to the editors and publishers of the following books and journals for giving me permission to reproduce parts of the following previously published material:

Journal of Child Psychology and Psychiatry, 'Two cases of developmental aphasia' (Miles, 1961).

The British Journal of Educational Psychology, 'More on dyslexia' (Miles, 1971).

Conventions

Throughout this book there are many examples of dyslexics' writings. These have been reproduced in roman type ('dsgib'), while correct spellings for words have been reproduced in italic type (*described*). When reproducing dyslexics' writings, I have striven to be as faithful to the original work as possible. Therefore, there are a few instances when a word had been crossed out by its writer; this crossing-out has been reproduced.

Lastly, since there are both male and female dyslexics, I have used the expression 'he or she' except when this would have been inelegant and clumsy. When I have quoted from my earlier publications, for instance Miles (1961), I have left 'he' and 'his' in place since at the time the matter was considered less important than it is now.

Part I Beginnings

1 Brenda

The scene: autumn 1949. Picture a newly appointed assistant lecturer, fresh from college and starting on an academic career. Apart from my normal teaching and research duties I was given the opportunity to attend the local Child Guidance Clinic for half a day a week. In those days the members of the clinical team comprised a psychiatrist, a psychologist and a psychiatric social worker. I was, of course, wholly new to the job. I had a degree in psychology but no postgraduate experience or training.

It was at this Child Guidance Clinic that my interest in dyslexia was first aroused. By a remarkable coincidence it was on my first day at the clinic that I met Brenda. Brenda was being referred at the age of 10 because of her poor progress in some aspects of her school work. She was being educated as a day girl at a private school not far from her home.

A report from her headmistress said, 'Appears very bright and is keen to answer in oral work, but ... she is very slow at any written work; possibly she is a little afraid of making mistakes. Her entire inability to spell is her great weakness.'

Tests given by myself and two colleagues showed Brenda to have an IQ of 116 on the Terman–Merrill (1937) test, a reading age of 8.3 years and a spelling age of 8.3 years on the Schonell (1945) reading and spelling tests, and a mental arithmetic age of 7.0 years on the Burt (1947) test. Her vocabulary score on the Terman–Merrill test (17 words correctly explained) gave her a pass at year xiv – far above the norm for her age. The incongruity of these results was clear, though it is interesting that at the time I had failed to appreciate the significance of her low score on the mental arithmetic test – the fact that there was a relationship between dyslexia and calculation difficulties did not become apparent to me until many years later.

Examination by an ophthalmologist revealed nothing defective in her eyesight and a psychiatric examination revealed no serious emotional difficulties. Some years ago, according to her mother, Brenda had confused 'b' and 'd', but this tendency had not persisted. Further tests at the clinic showed Brenda to be right-handed and right-eyed. In the light of the literature available at the time this was, perhaps, a surprising result: for many years the theory persisted that there was an association between dyslexia and 'crossed laterality', that is being right-handed and left-eyed or left-handed and right-eyed. However, my experiences with Brenda, and later with Michael (Chapter 2), led me to be somewhat sceptical from the start about whether there was any relationship between dyslexia and unusual handedness or eyedness (see also Miles, 1993a, Chapter 21, and Miles et al., 1996).

Even in the case of three-letter words she would hesitantly say, 'Is it right?' At one point she wrote, 'het' instead of *yet*; when shown the sentence again, she did not notice any mistake for about one minute, after which she said, 'I've put "het"', and corrected it. In my experience vertical confusions in dyslexics are not unknown, but, unlike horizontal ones – 'b'–'d' confusions in particular – they are rare.

Since I knew from the literature that some aphasic patients had difficulty in drawing a bicycle, I asked her to do so. For the same reason I also asked her if she could draw a ground plan of her house. Her attempts, as can be seen from my original paper (Miles, 1961, pp. 50–52), were extremely weird. It seems, however, that such curiosities are not typical of dyslexics in general, as I learned when I later gave these two tasks to other dyslexic children. At the time, of course, I had little idea of what was typical of the dyslexic child and what was not. Similarly she had appreciable difficulty over the Koh's Block test (a test similar to what afterwards became the Wechsler Block Design test), where two-dimensional patterns have to be reproduced by three-dimensional blocks, as in the Wechsler (1974) Block Design test. Most dyslexics do well on this item, but there are exceptions (Miles and Ellis, 1981, p. 230). What I would now say is that dyslexia is a variable syndrome: manifestations which have a dyslexic 'feel' to them vary from one individual to another.

Since in her spelling she frequently put the letters in the wrong order (see below), I had wondered if in some sense she 'saw' the letters the wrong way round – though I am still puzzled as to what exactly this might mean. With this idea in mind I asked her to copy written words from a book, writing as fast as she could; she was given to understand that it was a test of speed. When she was in a position to copy words, she made no errors at all. Her writing of letters in the wrong order when she spelled words could therefore not have been due to any kind of 'crossed pathways' in the optical system, such as had been hypothesised by Orton (1989).

During the testing Brenda occasionally tried out the 'look' of words on a rough piece of paper. This suggested an ability to compare the word in front of her with some kind of memorised visual image. I therefore thought it might be interesting to find out to what extent she had auditory imagery as well as visual imagery. When I asked her if she could imagine voices, she replied, 'I can imagine Daddy's – it's an odd voice.' She had no problem in understanding what I meant. I have found no evidence, either at that time or since, that dyslexics are in any way different from anyone else in respect of their visual or auditory imagery. Years later, when I gave the Bangor Dyslexia Test in 1982 (Miles, 1997) to some of my subjects, they did not physically turn in their seats but told me that they imagined themselves doing so. The ability to imagine appears to be in no way deficient in dyslexics.

Dr Simmons, the psychiatrist who was the head of the clinical team, explained to me that he thought Brenda was suffering from a form of aphasia. He believed that there were ways of helping such children with their reading and spelling, though he did not know exactly what needed to be done. He then asked me if I would like to try to give such help to Brenda. Unable to resist the bait, I agreed; and for the next nine months I used to visit her house once a week after school to give her spelling lessons. The sessions lasted for about 30 to 45 minutes.

One of my first tasks was to focus my attention on her spelling errors. I examined both the misspellings which I found in her school books, which were all less than a year old (see under '1'), and those which she had made on the Burt test when she was being tested at the clinic (see under '2').

This is what I found:

1 • whde like to go to es school whte Tome
  would like to go to school with Tom
 • a large bees of stfe calld a carpet
  a large piece of stuff called a carpet
 • cooking is den on the sotof
  cooking is done on the stove
 • the both is to be fond in the bothroom
  the bath is to be found in the bathroom
 • he whnet, and his sissder did the whsing
  he went, and his sister did the washing
 • she ackte
  she asked
 • ofar there
  over there
 • it is plasant to bathe and slebas in the sea when it is shmth and cam
  it is pleasant to bathe and splash in the sea when it is smooth and calm
 • we kach shreps
  we catch shrimps
 • wather is rogff and the spera lashes high in the air it is buter to whach the anger wafs from a safe disdons up the beech
  water is rough and the spray lashes high in the air it is better to watch the angry waves from a safe distance up the beach
 • prty calad catins
  pretty coloured curtains
 • he is a dag
  he is a dog

2 • I saw hre run by in the wet
  I saw her run by in the wet
 • A bird nets in the grss gress
  A bird's nest in the grass
 • The little kintton
  The little kitten
 • I have askt fourty girls ... noen falled
  I have asked forty girls ... none failed
 • Imatet there indosty
  Imitate their industry
 • Axsplan every santens
  Explain every sentence
 • The red hod fall on the wet mad
  The red bud fell on the wet mud

- My dog cut his lag on an opon tin
  My dog cut his leg on an open tin

It is clearly puzzling that such odd spelling mistakes should occur in the work of a girl who in some ways was clearly very intelligent. This was the basic challenge which was destined to affect my life for over fifty years.

I was given carte blanche by Dr Simmons to explore all possible methods of teaching. I decided to pay special attention to Brenda's spelling rather than to her reading. The programme which I devised for her was based on the assumption that she needed to pay close attention to the mouth movements – in particular the movements of her lips, tongue and vocal chords – when she said a word. It was then necessary for her to associate these movements with particular letters of the alphabet. This was what she had been trying to do already, but the matter was now made consciously explicit to her.

For all its oddity it is clear that her spelling is not unintelligent spelling. My hypothesis was that she was relying to a large extent on the tactile-kinaesthetic information resulting from her tongue and lip positions and movements when she pronounced the words. In other words it was first necessary for her to say the words either aloud or subvocally before she wrote them down, and her spelling was an attempt to put on paper the written symbols for tongue and lip positions and movements, not the written symbols for words as such.

It follows from this hypothesis that confusion between letters is most likely whenever the tactile-kinaesthetic cues are such as to make discrimination difficult. I therefore attempted to analyse her spelling with this consideration in mind.

Mistakes over vowels   In the first place little tactile-kinaesthetic information is obtainable by pronunciation of vowels; and it would therefore be evidence in support of our hypothesis if mistakes over vowels were relatively more numerous than mistakes over consonants. This is in effect what we find. Analysis of the above spelling gives the following table.

Table 1.1. Numbers of correct and incorrect spellings of consonants and vowels by Brenda

	Correct	Incorrect
Consonants	316	36
Vowels	160	58

Adapted from Miles (1961)

It is clear from this table that Brenda was making a larger proportion of errors over vowels than errors over consonants (note 1.1).

If we are dependent simply on the tactile-kinaesthetic data arising from tongue and lip positions and movements, it is often difficult to tell whether a vowel occurs or not. Our hypothesis therefore explains how it was that Brenda was able to string consonants together with no vowels at all and sometimes add vowels in the wrong place. Examples of the first type of mistake are 'stfe' and 'shmth', and of the second, 'spera', 'slebas' and 'sotof'.

Where the superfluous vowel is inserted, it is probable that Brenda was saying the word extra slowly. This may well have been the result of an attempt to be extremely careful, and it is worth calling attention to the large expenditure of effort which spelling involved for her. As I wrote at the time in my 1961 paper, 'We may be quite sure that for the developmental aphasic spelling is extremely hard work.'

The inclusion and omission of the letter 'e' appears for Brenda to have been a matter of guesswork. No doubt she had been told that some words carried the final mute 'e', but had no means of telling when it was or was not required. Thus she included an unwanted final 'e' in 'whde', 'whte', 'Tome', 'stfe' and 'ackte' and omitted a required final 'e' in 'bees' (*piece*) and 'sotof' (*stove*).

Mistakes over consonants   If our hypothesis is correct, one would expect all or most of the mistakes over consonants to occur when the tactile-kinaesthetic cues are least informative. This is in fact what we find. Three main classes of mistake will be considered first, namely (i) the substitution of an incorrect letter, (ii) the addition of an incorrect letter and (iii) the omission of a letter.

There are no tactile-kinaesthetic cues for distinguishing a soft 'c' from an 's' or a hard 'c' from a 'k'. This would explain why *catch* is spelt with a 'k' ('kach'), why 's' is substituted for 'c' in *distance* ('disdons') and *sentence* ('santens'), and why 'c' is substituted for 's' in one of the spellings of *asked* ('ackte'). The 'd' in *asked* is in fact pronounced as a 't', which would explain the substitution of 't' for 'd' in both 'ackte' and 'askt'); and substitution of 'd' for 't' in *distance* ('disdons') and *sister* ('sissder') is made particularly easy because of the s-sound immediately beforehand and the schwa sound which follows.

As regards position of the lips 'b' and 'p' are similar to each other as are 'f' and 'v'; in both cases the only differences are in voicing, and these are sometimes minimal. Examples of confusion over 'b' and 'p' are 'slebas' for *splash* and 'bees' for *piece*. Examples of confusion over 'f' and 'v' are 'ofar' for *over*, 'wafs' for *waves* and 'sotof' for *stove*. There is the further complication in this case that Brenda lived in Wales, where the v-sound is represented by a single 'f' and the f-sound by 'ff'. Even those who speak no Welsh may come across place names (e.g. Llanfairfechan) and notices (e.g. PREIFAT – private) where the 'v' sound is represented by an 'f'.

The examples cited in this section account for 14 out of the 36 mistakes.

The addition of 's' after 'x' in 'axsplan' (*explain*) is phonetically intelligible if we assume Brenda to have been saying the word slowly and carefully. The addition of 'h' after 'w', as in 'whde' (*would*), 'whte' (*with*), 'whnet' (*went*), 'whsing' (*washing*) and 'whach' (*watch*) is also understandable if we assume that she knew that in some cases 'w' would be followed by 'h'; in that case the absence of tactile-kinaesthetic data would make the decision whether to include or omit the 'h' a matter of guesswork. Few speakers are strict in sounding the 'h' in *where, what* etc.

The examples cited in this paragraph account for a further six out of the 36 mistakes.

There are no tactile-kinaesthetic cues for determining whether there are two *t*'s in *better*, two *f*'s in *stuff*, or two *l*'s in *failed*, nor are they represented by any very definite tongue or lip movements. This explains five out of the 36 mistakes.

Mistakes also occurred in connection with the letters 'l', 'm', 'n' and 'r'. Thus there is no cue to indicate the presence of an 'l' in *would* or in *calm* ('whde', 'cam'). The 'm' in *shrimps* is not a sound prominent in normal speech, which makes sense of Brenda's 'shreps'; and the converse to this appears to have happened when she put in the extra 'n' in *kitten* ('kintton') – presumably she knew that sometimes the extra 'm' or 'n' is needed even though it is not heard. The *r*'s in *coloured* and *curtains* are not represented in English by tongue or lip movements; hence we have 'calad' and 'catins'; 'indosty' for *industry* appears to be the result of rather slipshod pronunciation.

The examples in this paragraph explain a further seven mistakes.

'Rogff' for *rough* accounts for a further one. There remain the extra 'h' in *smooth* ('shmth'), the omission of 'h' in *splash* ('slebas') and 'a bird nets' for *a bird's nest*. In the case of 'a bird nets' it is not at all clear what has happened. It is possible that Brenda was confused and simply put in an 's' randomly without having time to work out where exactly it should go.

At first glance it might seem that Brenda's spelling is full of what at the time, following Orton (1937), I called 'reversals' – letters misplaced as a result of directional confusion. A closer examination, however, will, I think, reveal that there are relatively few clear-cut cases of this. Thus 'whte' and 'whsing' are not necessarily examples of a misplaced 'h'; the 'h' may simply have been added to the 'w' as in 'whde' and 'whach'. Even 'hre' for *her* may not be what Orton would have called a 'kinetic reversal'; the 'e' may simply be a mute 'e', as in 'stfe' and 'whde'; 'noen' for *none* is similarly ambiguous. To start the word *school* 'cs' clearly indicates some uncertainty over letter order, as does 'nets' for *nest*, but putting letters in the wrong order need not imply 'kinetic reversals' in Orton's sense (see also Chapter 3, comment no. 3).

Since the main problem for Brenda was that of determining the correct vowel, I directed my energies in the first place to trying to find a way of helping her over this. To start off, she was required to draw five columns in an exercise book. The first was headed by the word *bag*, the second by the word *beg* and the third, fourth and fifth by the words *big, bog* and *bug*. Each column had a 'noise', which was its vowel sound with the consonants on either side being removed. Using the International Phonetic Association (IPA) script it is possible to symbolise these five noises as æ, e, ɪ, ɒ and ʌ.

Brenda was asked to make the 'noises' for each column in turn, concentrating on the mouth movements as she did so. The 'noise' could easily be associated with a particular letter, and thus any word with the same 'noise' as, say, *bag* would necessarily have to have the same letter, namely 'a', as its vowel. *Cat, ham* etc. would go in the *bag* column; *cot, dog* etc. would go in the *bog* column, and so on. The consonants were left in the main to look after themselves since, apart from 'f' and 'v' and a few other pairs, the phonetic distinction between them is not difficult to make.

The next stage was to introduce a new set of 'noises'. The 'noises' chosen were the long 'a', the long 'i' and the long 'o' (IPA script, eɪ, aɪ, əʊ) and the three columns were headed by the words *tame, time* and *tome*. Brenda was required to pay attention to the contrast between the 'noise' æ (short 'a') and the eɪ 'noise' (long 'a'), and was told that when the long vowel occurred an 'e' was necessary at the end. Thus *mate* carries a final 'e', whereas *mat* does not. (Only three columns were introduced into her book here. Columns corresponding to the long 'e' and the long 'u' could have been made (iː and uː)), to allow for words such as *gene* and *tune*, but this seemed an unjustifiable complication at this early stage since most words with the iː 'noise' are not spelled 'e-blank-e', and words ending 'u-blank-e' are not only few but sometimes have different pronunciations, e.g. *tune* and *fluke*. At the present stage simplicity was essential.

Further 'noises' were introduced in a systematic way – 'ai' and 'oa', as in *pain* and *moat*, and words ending in 'ea' and 'ee', such as *sea* and *see*. Brenda was told that she would simply have to remember which words went like *pain* and which like *tape*, which like *moat* and which like *hope*, which like *sea* and which like *see*, etc. I explained that in these cases she might sometimes be unlucky and guess wrong, but this would not be her fault, provided she set about the task in the way I had taught her.

In due course I introduced her to words ending in 'ay' and 'ight' and also to 'oo', 'ou' and 'oi'. At this point it was possible to introduce words containing more than one syllable, such as *avoid* and *loiter*, as were words ending in the suffix '-ation'. Once Brenda had become familiar with the suffix '-ation', it was possible for her to spell much longer words – provided they were regular – such as *procrastination* or *contamination*.

In general the purpose was to give her rules to follow whenever this was possible, rather than present her with the formidable task of having to remember every word in the language by heart.

As far as Brenda was concerned the method had its ups and downs. She seemed to take to both the method and the teacher satisfactorily, but progress was by no means uniform. Thus one report, six months from the start, reads: 'Evening of despair. Brenda had a cold, which may account for some of it. Even so she showed remarkable disability. Starting with "point" she could not even make the "oi" "noise". We went laboriously through other words that I had put on a list, with Brenda guessing wildly at the 'p' and 'e' correct noises. "Pain" was started with the letters 'p' and 'e'. Definite relapse … we shall never get far at this rate.' The report for the next week, however, is more encouraging: 'Brenda much brighter again this evening. Cold better. Went through last time's list without much trouble.'

An incidental difficulty with the method used (quite apart from its failure to allow for the many irregularities in the English language) is that vowels are pronounced differently in different regions. Brenda was not alone in finding *bag* and *beg*, as pronounced by me, hard to distinguish.

At one point, towards the end of the teaching sessions, Brenda was asked to place her tongue on her upper lip and to spell without using either of them. This does not, of course, eliminate altogether the possibility of cues derived from mouth movements, or of images of mouth movements, but it is a restriction which would be expected, if my main thesis about her spelling is correct, to make matters very difficult for her. She immediately said: 'This is cruel', and among other misspellings she produced 'imagention' for *imagination*, 'armodelo' for *armadillo*, 'amatomegal' for *anatomical* and 'buciful' for *beautiful*. At the same session I questioned her directly about her progress. She explained that she could see the words now in a way in which she could not before. 'It just came. I can see them in my brain's eye (sic); before I was just guessing.'

The teaching sessions were discontinued after about nine months owing to her family's change of home. Unfortunately no final spelling test was given as a check on her improvement, but a year and a half later, in reply to a follow-up by the Child Guidance Clinic, her headmistress wrote: 'Her form mistress says that she has made steady (although not spectacular) progress in spelling and seems quite hopeful about her.'

The following extract from her school work was obtained:

> An Adventure out at sea
> We had decided to go on a boat for a week. We packed our things, and ordered a boat. Next day we were off ... It was about four o'clock, when we arrived, so we got tea rightaway. Ann, our friend was putting a cake on the cloth, when she slipped and disappeared. We called, and called, but we could not fined her. Worried and firghtened we ran over the green slopes calling all the time, but we could not fined her.
>
> We made our way done to the beach, but as we arrived there we found Ann's sandals on the sands, and foot prints round about. Trumbling with firghten we followed the prints, thouth I did not want to, but follow them we did. The led us to a cave covered with seaweed. We pulled the seaweed down, and there was Ann tirde to a roack. Hurriedly we untired her, only to find three men there.
>
> Roslie told us to run. Run we did, and reched the Police taytion looking like scarecrows with seaweed hanging frome us. We told the Police, who run up and court the men. We recived a big rewurd.

I shall return in Chapter 3 to a discussion of some of the theoretical issues raised by Brenda's case. A lesson which I learned from the very start was that, if children such as Brenda are to be helped, it is necessary to carry out a thorough and detailed examination of their spelling errors.

RECOLLECTIONS

On one occasion I remember telling a colleague of Welsh birth that Brenda could not easily hear the difference between *bag* and *beg*. He replied that, as I had said the two words, he could not hear any difference either! He was a native Welshman, and I think his difficulty may have been caused by my unfamiliar pronunciation. I was told later by my colleague E.L. Tibbits, Lecturer in Speech Education, that, in north Wales, if I had said 'baag' the sound would have been picked out more easily.

NOTE

Note 1.1   Chi-squared $(df\,1) = 26.23$, $p < 0.001$.

2 Michael

Michael was referred to the Bangor Child Guidance Clinic at the age of nine years nine months. His extreme weakness at reading and spelling had already caused his parents concern, and they wished for further investigation. I myself was not responsible for his original testing, but as his teacher I had ample opportunity thereafter for observing his behaviour.

His test results were:

> WISC verbal IQ: 116
> Performance IQ: 129 (Wechsler, 1949)
> Terman–Merrill IQ: 128 (Terman and Merrill, 1937)
> Schonell Graded Word Reading test: reading age 5.3 (Schonell and Schonell, 1952)

No spelling age was given, but when he took the Burt (1947) Dictation test he produced the following:

> Mi deg cet his lug on an open ten
> It is on a cat bot nat a deg
> I sra har ran bie in the wet
> she cam to sec ro steal a bac net in the gar the crul lacl cen

The psychologist who originally tested Michael thought that absence from school and some learning inhibition due to emotional causes might be sufficient to account for Michael's weakness at reading and spelling. Even at the time, however, and with my very limited knowledge of dyslexia this seemed to me unlikely. His parents certainly showed some anxiety, but not a disproportionate amount in the circumstances. A psychiatric interview led Dr Simmons to conclude: 'I could find no good evidence of maladjustment of a kind that would warrant concern.'

I started on a teaching programme along similar lines to that which I had used in the case of Brenda. Michael was gradually introduced to the 'noises' made by the different vowel sounds. In addition I invented sentences requiring a knowledge of the 'noises' which he had already learned, but with no irregular words.

More stress, however, was laid in Michael's case on reading as well as on spelling. For the next eight months Michael came to the clinic once per week (with occasional absences owing to illness or around Christmas and Easter). At the end of eight months his reading age on the Schonell Word Recognition test (Schonell and Schonell, 1952) had gone up to 7.1, an increase of one year nine and a half months.

After a period at boarding school he returned about eight months later for more teaching. At this point I gave him the Schonell Word Recognition test again, and his score was 7.7. This suggested that even without special teaching his reading ability was at least holding its own, so to speak, with his chronological age. For about the next eight months he received fairly intensive tuition, usually for three periods a week instead of the one period which he had received earlier. At this time Michael was aged between nine and 10.

One of the things which I particularly noticed was that during his reading, as well as during his spelling, he was mixing up 'b' with 'd' and 'p' with 'q'. Table 2.1 provides examples of these and other errors.

Table 2.1. Some examples of Michael's reading errors

Target word	Read by him as
on	no
pot	top
Ben	der ... (pause)
quickly	p- p- (pause)
dog	bog
been	den–done
quickly	properly
boys	boys, no, dogs
was	saw
for	of

Adapted from Miles (1961)

At one point I called his attention to 'p' and 'q' and 'b' and 'd' and asked him to imitate their spatial direction with his hands. He said, ' "p" goes this way and "q" this way.' But in his first demonstration he did it the wrong way round. Later, however, I noted, 'He has at last grasped the difference between "quickly" and "properly".'

During later sessions, when he was aged about 11, and I could ask him to spell long words such as 'discrimination', I found that in the case of four- or five-syllable words he could not even say them without confusion, let alone spell them. Thus he is reported in my notes as having been very much tied up over the words 'imagination' and 'conflagration'. He was clearly trying hard, but the word just would not come right!

It was not until many years later that I realised that becoming 'tied up' when saying certain long words could be an indicator of dyslexia. I then included the request to repeat some suitable words as part of the Bangor Dyslexia Test (Miles, 1997).

I also had access to his school books. Figure 2.1 is a reproduction of some work in his own handwriting.

In many of my talks I have presented this reproduction to local Dyslexia Associations and other organisations as an illustration of how a highly intelligent boy can nevertheless produce weird and inconsistent spellings.

To form part of the present chapter I have also transcribed some other extracts from his school books.

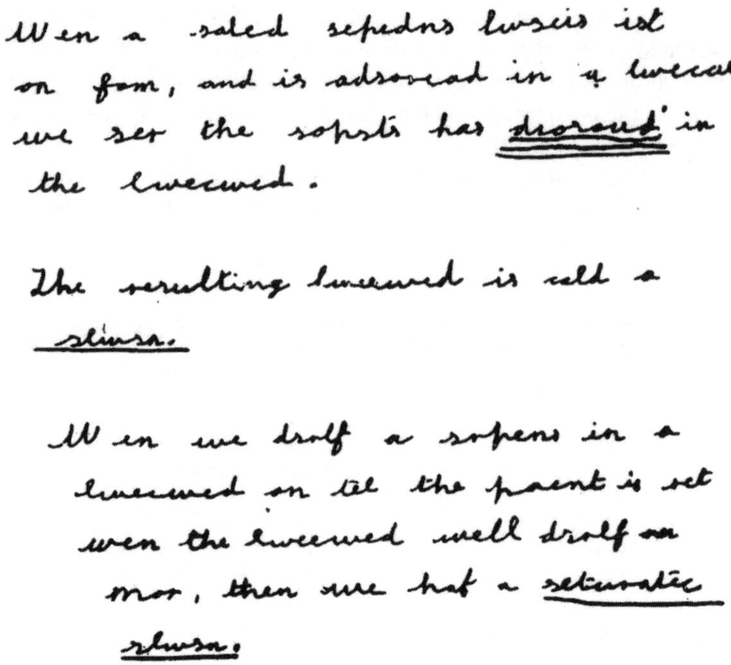

When a solid substance loses its own form, and is absorbed in a liquid, we say the substance has dissolved in the liquid. The resulting liquid is called a solution. When we dissolve a substance in a liquid until the point is reached when the liquid will dissolve no more, then we have a saturated solution.

Figure 2.1.   A sample of Michael's handwriting.

1. Latitude is macad desdns NS of the cwat. Aparl of latitude thit runs fow all the plas that aer at the same desdns macad NS of the rcaudr.
   Latitude is measured distance NS of the equator. A parallel of latitude [is a line] that runs through all the places that are at the same distance measured NS of the equator.
2. How things flot. A thing flots, if it can pas auva a naf lecwed, and not be cafad. Gafate and the lecwed pajing the obsect up, helps a thing to flot, becas the Gafate is paling the obsect dawn, and the lccwed is pasing it up.
   How things float. A thing floats, if it can pass over enough liquid, and not be covered. Gravity and the liquid pushing the object up helps a thing to float because gravity is pulling the object down, and the liquid is pushing it up.
3. D sgib Surface Tension. Surface Tension is lace a sgen go the lecwed, bat the is not a sgen at all, it is jest Gafate and the pasing of the lecwed. (The correct spelling of 'surface tension' is surprising, and my surmise is that the words had been written for him on the blackboard.)
   Describe Surface Tension. Surface tension is like a skin on the liquid, but there is not a skin at all; it is just gravity and the pushing of the liquid.

4. Ien filings. Ien filings aer lecl peses of Ien, and we pat sam in the water, and sum of them boc fou the amajnae sgen and sam amand.

Iron filings. Iron filings are little pieces of iron, and we put some in the water, and some of them broke through the imaginary skin and some remained.

5. The negl. We pat a Negl in the water, fast we pat a pes of blating papa in the water, and pat the Negl on it and the papa sanɔ and the Negl acded an the Surface Tension.

The Needle. We put a needle in the water; first we put a piece of blotting paper in the water, and put the needle on it; and the paper sank and the needle acted on the surface tension.

Michael's difficulty in producing the correct vowel was, if anything, more severe than Brenda's. The results of an analysis of the errors which he made in the dictation test at his first assessment are set out in Table 2.2 below.

It can be seen from this table that, as in Brenda's case, there is a significantly higher proportion of vowel errors than of consonant errors (note 2.1). In the first three lines the only mistake over a consonant is 'sra' for *saw* – which represents one mistake in 37 consonants as compared with 11 mistakes out of 16 in the case of vowels. The other 13 consonant errors are made up mostly of omissions.

Examination of the extracts from Michael's school books shows many of the same features that were found in Brenda's case, e.g. 'c' for 's' in 'macad' (*measured*) and 'pes' (*piece*), 'sd' for 'st' in 'desdns' (*distance*), 'f' for 'v' in 'dsolf' (*dissolve*), 'cafad' (*covered*) and 'gafate' (*gravit*) and 'd' for 't' in 'acded' (acted).

Other similar confusions are 'sg' for 'sc' or 'sk', as in 'dsgib' (*describe*) and 'sgen' (*skin*). In some cases the spelling corresponds to pronunciation at rather an infantile level, e.g. 'negl' for *needle* and 'lecl' for *little*.

In addition the letter 'c' is reversed ('sanɔ' for *sank*; there is 'on' for *no*, and other misplacing of letters, e.g. 'ist' for *its* and 'sepedns' for *substance*.

Finally his attempts at *liquid* seem to show a struggle followed by a result with which he was presumably fairly well satisfied, 'lwcae', 'lwecwed' and 'lecwed'. The final result is in fact by far the nearest of the three to the actual sound of the word (lɪkwɪd). It is difficult for those of us who are adequate spellers to realise what hard work it must have been for Michael to accomplish even this degree of correctness.

My lessons with Michael came to an end when he went away to a different boarding school. About a year later his parents reported that, though still weak at spelling, he was now a very adequate reader. Reflecting on Michael's case I was still not

Table 2.2. Number of correct and incorrect consonants and vowels in a sample of Michael's spelling

	Correct	Incorrect
Consonants	64	14
Vowels	30	19

Adapted from Miles (1961)

satisfied with the explanation offered by my colleague (see above) that absences from school and parental pressures were sufficient to account for the problems: there would in that case have been an impossible mismatch between cause and effect. The cause, as in Brenda's case, had to be constitutional in origin.

NOTE

Note 2.1   Chi-squared = 6.569, $p < 0.02$.

3 Thoughts on Brenda and Michael

My next task was to examine my findings on Brenda and Michael and try to make sense of them. After some delay I was able to submit a paper for publication (Miles, 1961), and, after suitable refereeing, the editor accepted it (note 3.1).

I entitled the paper 'Two cases of developmental aphasia'. The term 'developmental aphasia' was one which had been used by Macmeeken (1939), and although it has now been superseded I still believe it to be of theoretical interest; this is because it provides a link with acquired aphasia. This link is important not least because one can now be confident that the behaviour which I was describing has a constitutional basis – that some sort of deficiency in the physiological mechanisms for language is at work and that this was the main causal factor in creating Brenda's and Michael's literacy problems.

To illustrate my thinking at the time I shall now quote extracts from the theoretical parts of my paper (Miles, 1961). I have done some editing and left out some parts of the paper which do not now seem relevant. In essentials, however, I believe that the approach which I adopted at the time is a useful one. At the end of the chapter I have included some comments written in the light of my subsequent experiences. Where the letters (A), (B) etc. appear in brackets these refer to the comments which appear at the end of this chapter in the section 'Comments in retrospect'.

INTRODUCTION

Although the terminology is in some confusion there is little doubt that a concept is needed for referring to a certain specific syndrome (that is cluster of symptoms) displayed by an appreciable number of children whose reading and spelling ability falls short of their intelligence. Among educationalists in general the problem deserves more attention, in my opinion, than it has so far received.

In the present paper I wish the term 'aphasia' to be understood in a wide sense. By derivation it means simply 'not speaking', but it is nowadays used to indicate a whole range of disorders of speech and language. In speaking of 'developmental' aphasia I am contrasting it, as did Macmeeken (1939), with 'acquired' aphasia. The appropriate powers of recognition and spatial orientation (A) which occur in normal children in the course of development have in these cases temporarily failed to mature; and while aphasic symptoms in the adult can usually be attributed beyond reasonable doubt to some specific injury, e.g. brain-damage resulting from a bullet wound, in the case of children suffering from 'developmental' aphasia this is not so, and there is no record of any acquired injury.

It would have been possible, of course, to refer to the syndrome by some purely neutral term, e.g. 'the omega syndrome', and in so doing one would be making the minimum possible commitment on the theoretical side. In taking over the phrase 'developmental aphasia' I have deliberately chosen to go further than this. I wish to imply that our understanding of these disabilities in children can be helped by an examination of the whole group of aphasic disabilities in adults. Although there may be no history of actual brain damage, in the sense of injury, in the case of these children, their performance is sufficiently similar to that of brain-damaged adults to make us suspect an analogous failure of cortical function. By convention all terms such as 'aphasia', 'apraxia', 'dyslexia' etc. are assumed to carry the theoretical implication that they are caused by some neurological failure of function, and I have deliberately chosen a term with this implication. Thus to say that a child suffers from developmental aphasia is not, as some have supposed, simply a highfalutin way of saying that he is weak at reading; it is to postulate an identifiable syndrome and link its manifestations with those displayed by brain-damaged adults.

To avoid all possible misunderstanding I should make clear that in labelling a child a 'developmental aphasic' I am very far indeed from implying that he cannot be helped. What I have in mind is a behavioural label with physiological implications; this is perfectly compatible with the view that the practising teacher can learn more from behavioural descriptions than from physiological ones. My objection to the use of a behavioural label *simpliciter* is that in using it we are overlooking the analogies with adult aphasia, and thereby gratuitously depriving ourselves of the chance of increased theoretical understanding. To refuse to classify phenomena at all on the grounds of their diversity is surely to give up the scientific ghost altogether. In general I would say that the main difference between those who assert and those who deny the existence of developmental aphasia lies in the degree to which they are prepared to commit themselves theoretically. It seems to me an obvious requirement for scientific progress that our concepts should be as theory-laden as possible; it is better to say something and be proved wrong – and I would stress that my conclusions in this paper are tentative and exploratory – than not to say anything at all.

SOME THEORETICAL IMPLICATIONS

One of the main points which seems to me to be established by the cases of Brenda and Michael and similar ones is that there is a specific disability *sui generis*, as opposed to an ordinary manifestation of dullness or stupidity. Macmeeken (1939) has shown that developmental aphasia can occur in children of high intelligence, and this finding receives further confirmation from the cases of both Brenda (IQ 116+) and Michael (IQ 116–128) (B). Indeed it is more likely to be noticeable in children of high intelligence, since the discrepancy between their performance on the majority of tasks and their performance on tasks involving their specific disability is all the more marked.

What is of particular interest and difficulty is to indicate just what it is (or what is the main thing) which the developmental aphasic cannot do. There are, of course, the reversals (C) of letters and words and the tendency to become 'tied up' in saying long words (both very pronounced in Michael), and there is the constructional apraxia (D), which was very pronounced in Brenda (C). The main difficulty, however, which they both shared, was a special sort of failure in word recognition. This failure resulted not only in poor reading ability but also in extreme difficulty in spelling, together with a complete failure to recognise if their effort was right or wrong. I shall attempt in what follows to throw further light on the question of what this failure involves.

THE CONCEPT OF WORD-BLINDNESS

Hinshelwood (1917) writes of 'word-blindness'. This must presumably be taken as a metaphor, since the children are certainly not blind in the normal sense, as Hinshelwood himself agrees (1917, p. 2). Any child who cannot recognise a word is to that extent 'blind' in a sense, but this tells us nothing. Indeed the term 'word-blindness' has been criticised (like the term 'dyslexia') for being an unnecessary and even misleading way of saying that the child cannot read – unnecessary because it adds nothing, and misleading because the word 'blindness' suggests a permanent and perhaps incurable state. Yet it is surely significant that Hinshelwood wanted to use the metaphor, and we may well ask if there is not something which the child cannot 'see' in some sense. What exactly is the connection between this disability and vision?

THREE SUGGESTED ANALOGIES

A possible analogy would be the following experiment. Suppose that the subject places his hand downwards on a table and that the observer writes words on the back of it with a pencil (E). The subject is then asked to 'read' by tactile-kinaesthetic cues what is written there. The result of this experiment is what might be expected. The subject can feel something on his hand (just as the developmental aphasic can see something on the paper) but cannot without practice organise what he feels into a meaningful whole. Now to speak of numbness or insensitivity here seems to be wrong in much the same way as it is wrong to describe the developmental aphasic as 'word-blind'; it is rather that the subject in this experiment cannot operate symboli- cally with tactile data, just as the developmental aphasic cannot operate symbolically with visual data.

Another possible analogy would be with our failure to grasp sentences as meaning- ful wholes if the letters are simply read out in succession. Thus, without practice, it would not be easy to grasp the significance of the auditory stimuli which for purposes of this paper may be visually represented as: 'tee' 'aitch' 'ee' 'see' 'ay' 'tee' 'ess' 'ay' 'tee' 'oh' 'en' 'tee' 'aitch' 'ee' 'em' 'ay' 'tee'.

It should be noted that in both these two analogies the different parts of the stimu- lus are presented successively; there is therefore to that extent a difference from the visual word where the different parts of the stimulus are present simultaneously. If these two analogies are valid, we must say that the act of integration which most people find difficult in the case of successive stimuli is difficult for the developmental aphasic even in the case of vision.

The most satisfactory analogy, however, is, I think, that of the word which loses its meaning if we repeat it sufficiently often. This phenomenon is so familiar, and, to my mind, so important, that it is surprising that such scant attention has been paid to it by psychologists (F). I have not so far attempted any systematic experimentation; but we can, I think, take it as a matter of common experience that if we repeat a word, say, 10 or 20 times in immediate succession that word ceases to have any mean- ing for us. What happens here appears to be the converse of what happens in certain patients with acquired aphasia (Head, 1926). Unable to produce, say, the word 'key' when presented with a key, they revert to circumlocutions, e.g. 'You unlock doors with it'; their problem is finding the right name for a visually presented object.

It seems, then, for the developmental aphasic that the visual symbol fails to carry any meaning; it is as meaningless as the word 'key' when one has repeated it 20 times.

MACMEEKEN'S DESCRIPTION

Macmeeken (1939, p.25) writes: 'The suggestion arises ... that for these children ... no word exists to be recognised until the child has rendered his written symbol in terms of the spoken word.' This seems to me a difficult but interesting statement of the problem. What is meant by saying that a word does or does not 'exist to be recognised'? Perhaps the following points may clarify the position. When a normal person (G) recognises, say, the written word *dog*, we must suppose that this written word acts as a stimulus to 'touch off' one or more responses appropriate to dogs; these responses would be similar to those produced as a result of the auditory stimulus word *dog* and to those produced by the actual presence of a dog. In that case we could say that the word *dog* exists to be recognised; a feeling of familiarity attaches to it at sight. In the case of these children there is no such feeling of familiarity, or at any rate such a feeling of familiarity does not come easily. The appropriate responses are touched off only when the written symbol is converted into some other form, e.g. in terms of tongue and lip positions and movements or in terms of tactile-kinaesthetic memory ('tracing the word in the air'). As Macmeeken (1939) writes, 'Such effort is in many cases accompanied by exaggerated tongue and lip movements, movements of the head, facial grimaces, even by other body movements, say, of arm or leg' (H). It seems as though the visual letters will not fuse into a word, but that, at least in the case of intelligent children, they can be mouthed into forming a word. Similarly when a child is required to reproduce the word in writing, this creates particular difficulty since the feedback of combined visual letters does not convey meaning, as it does in the case of a normal reader, and the only way of obtaining feedback is to convert the individual letters into tongue and lip movements. In the case of Brenda this seems to have been precisely what was happening.

The objection may be raised that Brenda sometimes tried out the 'look' of words on rough paper; does not this suggest that after all she does have some visual memory for words? If my suggested view of the case is correct, it would seem to follow that the written word has no symbolic function for her; the letters d-o-g are a thing – a 'word-dog' one might say – which, when spoken together, indicate that one has mentioned the word *dog*. One recognises a word – in this case the word *dog* – by its general shape, and once one knows the shape one can compare one's written word with it. The difficulty is that the shape of words of more than three letters is very complex; we should expect failure on any but the shortest words, and this is precisely what we find. The fact that a person tries out the 'look' of words is thus quite compatible with saying that the visual word is not functioning as a symbol.

The child is not therefore 'rendering his written symbol in terms of the spoken word', as Macmeeken (1939, p. 25) says; he is converting a non-symbolic mark on paper letter by letter into some other form in such a way that the end product in its new form can function as a symbol. It is a laborious way of achieving what non-aphasic children can achieve much more easily.

If we take the essential features in the syndrome to be reversals (C) and failure at word recognition, the question arises as to how the two are related. This is a matter which seems to me very difficult, and what follows is put forward as speculation only. If it is correct that successive presentation of parts of a word (e.g. the auditory presentation of the noises 'see' 'ay' 'tee', see earlier) makes integration more difficult than if the parts of the word are given simultaneously as in vision, can it be that something analogous to successive presentation occurs in the case of developmental aphasics even when the visual word is involved? I am not of course suggesting that there is any failure of integration when **things** lie side by side, but only when **symbols** lie side by side. It seems to me not impossible that the visual perception of **symbols** should be disordered temporally as well as spatially, and this would create in the case of vision the same problems of integration as the rest of us have in the case of the 'successive' senses of hearing and touch. It is because of a failure of temporal integration that the visual word seems unfamiliar, and it is because vision is involved that one is tempted to speak of word-**blindness**. The connection with vision, however, is a de facto one, arising because visual symbols for normal people, unlike auditory or tactual ones, allow integration to be made with all the parts present simultaneously. The result of spatial and temporal disorientation is to affect vision rather than the other senses (I).

There are, in fact, many interesting analogies between spatial and temporal awareness; this was pointed out in particular in the eighteenth century by the philosopher Immanuel Kant (note 3.2), and it is therefore not unreasonable to suppose that the same cortical failure can affect both.

THE PSYCHOANALYTIC APPROACH

It is suggested by Blanchard (1946) that in a certain proportion of cases, perhaps 20 per cent, reading disability is a symptom of an underlying neurotic anxiety. She does not dispute that there may be many cases where there is emotional disturbance resulting from the failure at reading, but her special concern is with those cases where the neurotic anxiety is itself a causal factor. In such cases it would seem that improvement at reading is difficult or impossible without an adequate working through of the unconscious fantasies which underlie the neurosis.

In one of Blanchard's examples a boy is reported both as reversing letters and as combining them in odd ways. In explanation Blanchard calls attention to the view shared by most child analysts that words can be a means of displaying aggression. The behaviour in this particular case was indicative, according to Blanchard, of the boy's feelings towards his mother. The boy, we are told, was Jewish (on his father's side, presumably), whereas his mother was not. In the case of the reversals his purpose was aggressive, namely to attack her by writing in Hebrew; 'he tried to turn the English taught at school into Hebrew by writing it backwards' (Blanchard, 1946, p. 180). The other errors, in which he combined letters into what seemed nonsense, 'were symbolic of the love he still felt for his mother'. We are told, for instance, that he wrote: 'As ur mor' for *Ask your mother.* The boy also did what he called 'Chinese writing', which consisted of peculiar marks on paper. 'His "Chinese Writing" was a magic spell that would cause his mother to be tortured with sharp knives' (Blanchard, 1946, p. 181).

With regard to the 'Chinese writing', Blanchard unfortunately gives no examples. It would have been interesting to know if the 'peculiar marks' which she describes were ever actual letters, and whether they could have been genuine attempts to spell.

What is puzzling here is that both the reversals and the faulty spelling seem exactly comparable to those of Brenda and Michael as described in this paper. Unfortunately Blanchard does not give us details of whether and how the boy verbalised these alleged fantasies. If he did, one wonders if conceivably his remarks about writing in Hebrew could have arisen as an imaginative flight of fancy resulting from an **already existing** disability. In that case what happened was that the boy found himself, like other developmental aphasics, unable to spell, and then produced an imaginative story to explain it. We cannot tell on the evidence available.

What is crucial is this. The symptoms are so similar to those of Brenda and Michael that there are very strong prima facie grounds for looking for the same explanation in all three cases. If so, and if Blanchard's explanation is correct, it would follow that the weakness of both Brenda and Michael was due to some similar set of fantasies rather than primarily to any failure of cortical development. Unfortunately it is very difficult in practice to distinguish between the two hypotheses, since the improvement in Blanchard's boy could have been due to development, and the improvement in Brenda and Michael could have been due to the therapeutic effects of remedial teaching. It is worth noting that in Brenda's case she is reported as being in rather an excitable mood and as 'chaffing' her remedial teacher, and if the psychoanalytic approach to this type of disability is correct, it would follow that this incident, as part of a wider transference relationship, was of crucial importance.

However, there was no evidence in either case of any gross psychiatric disturbance, and I reached the conclusion that emotional maladjustment was not the main causal determinant (J).

SOME PRACTICAL IMPLICATIONS

If the main ideas expressed in this paper are correct, it follows that this type of disability is entirely beyond the child's control. This has important practical consequences for the handling of such cases. Both Brenda and Michael were able to appreciate and accept the fact that, for them personally, certain tasks were more difficult than for some of their contemporaries. For most of the time during the remedial teaching sessions they were prepared to make an effort; in special circumstances, e.g. when Brenda had a cold, making the effort was more difficult. A knowledge of these limitations enabled me to see how much could reasonably be expected of them at any particular time. There were times with Michael when I made clear that the required piece of reading or spelling was something within his power provided he was careful and followed the rules that I had given him. If he failed to be careful, I made clear that I expected him to do better, but where words were irregular or the rules which I had given him did not operate, there was no question of my finding fault with him or even expressing disappointment. What was necessary for me was to know when to say 'This is difficult – have a shot' and when to make clear that a particular task was within his power. If a child of this kind likes to be told whether he has done well or done badly, all that the teacher need do, to give an honest answer, is to adjust his standards of what constitutes doing well or doing badly in a special way on the basis of what a developmental aphasic can be expected to do.

A further point is this. On the assumption that developmental aphasia is a disability *sui generis*, it follows that figures obtained from many of the standard intelligence tests are liable to be under-estimations of the child's potential. The Terman–Merrill test, for instance, taps many abilities (this is one of the fascinating things about its use in practice), and includes items which the developmental aphasic is likely to find difficult (K).

In addition it should be remembered that among children of less ability the condition is more likely to pass unnoticed, since the discrepancy between reading ability and general brightness would be much less marked.

Finally, although I have suggested that the reason for developmental aphasia will ultimately be found to lie in a failure of function of the brain, it by no means follows that this failure of function will be permanent. The brain is in many ways altogether unlike a telephone system: if a telephone wire is broken, communication to a particular house is impossible, and there is no more to be said. The brain, on the other hand, is a very plastic organ, and even when there is definite damage to a particular area, as in acquired aphasia, another area can partially take over certain functions. In the case of developmental aphasia, where there is not so much damage as some failure of development, there is every prospect of fresh skills emerging. Individual attention is necessary for these children, and helping them to overcome their disability may be a lengthy and even painful process, but it seems from the data available that there is a good chance of successful progress.

COMMENTS IN RETROSPECT

(A) Macmeeken (1939, p. 27) describes the syndrome as one of 'directional confusion', and this clearly influenced the writing of the above passage. I would not now place the same emphasis on spatial orientation, since from the early 1970s it became clear that dyslexia is primarily a difficulty with certain aspects of language and symbolisation, rather than a difficulty over orientation.

(B) From the wording of this passage it seems that I was willing to use language which endorses somewhat uncritically the concept of IQ. It is clear, however, from what follows later in the paper that I was already aware of some of the difficulties when this concept is applied to dyslexic children (see also Chapter 9).

(C) I have retained the word 'reversal' as it was in my original paper. I now believe, however, that this word implies a mistaken theory of what is going on. Orton (1989) distinguishes what he calls 'static reversals', for instance 'b' in place of 'd' or 'p' in place of 'q', from what he calls 'kinetic reversals', which involve reversing the order of the letters, for instance by writing 'dna' in place of *and* or 'tworrom' in place of *tomorrow*. Some of his examples of 'kinetic reversals' could, I think, be explained not by a directional problem over left and right but by a failure to remember the order in which the letters should be written.

Also some of the so-called 'static reversals' involve reading or writing the mirror image of the correct word, for instance 'on' for *no* as well as 'b' for 'd' and 'p' for 'q'. As a result the expression 'mirror writing' found its way into the dyslexia literature and Orton even speculates that some dyslexics were extra gifted at it. However, the only hard evidence which has come my way suggests that this is not so. In Miles *et al.* (2001), in which my colleagues and I examine the mathematical abilities of 10-year-old children, there is an item which involves the decoding of mirror writing. Eighty-three per cent of 6 333 normal achievers answered the question correctly, but only 48% of 269 dyslexics of the same intelligence level did. This result does not surprise me in view of the cognitive complexity of tasks involving the decoding of mirror writing, and, given our present knowledge of dyslexia, I can think of no reason why anyone should now suppose that a dyslexic would find this task easy (note 3.3).

Orton's ideas in this area, though ingenious, seemed to me to have steered dyslexia research in the wrong direction. This is in no way to dispute the importance of the phenomena to which he called attention but only the theoretical superstructure which he brought in to explain them. In particular I cannot help wondering if the importance of the analogy of the mirror for our understanding of dyslexia has been exaggerated. I have heard lecturers speak in the same sentence of reversing 'b' and 'd' and reversing 'was' and 'saw'. However, although 'b' is the mirror image of 'd', 'was' is not the mirror image of 'saw'. I do not doubt that Orton was aware of this, but some of his successors appear to have been less cautious.

In Miles (1961) I follow Orton's theory by describing Michael's 'b'–'d' and 'p'–'q' confusions as 'reversals'. However, the word 'reversal' now seems to me to have misleading theoretical overtones. It is not clear to me that a child who has written 'b' for 'd' has **reversed** anything. I now prefer to say simply that the child has written the wrong letter. This avoids commitment to any theory as to why the mistake occurred. Similarly, although in fact 'b' is the mirror image of 'd', I am not sure that it helps to say that a child who writes 'b' for 'd' is doing 'mirror writing'.

(D) In publications later than Miles (1961) I have not had occasion to use the expression 'constructional apraxia'. Later experience has suggested to me that Brenda's attempts to draw a bicycle and a ground plan of her house are atypical of dyslexics in general. In the early 1960s I asked some of my subjects to draw a bicycle, but there were no particularly striking results. My problem at this stage of the research was to discover which of the things that I noticed in individual children were genuinely part of the dyslexic syndrome and which were only a characteristic of one particular individual. In contrast, becoming 'tied up' when attempting to say long words turned out to be an important feature in dyslexia, one which was tested for in the Bangor Dyslexia Test (Miles, 1997).

(E) The ability to recognise what is written on the hand is termed 'graphaesthesia' and has now been the subject of systematic study. A graphaesthesia test was used in the British Births Cohort Study (which I refer to in Chapters 19 and 20), and Mary Haslum and I have recently been examining some of the results (Haslum and Miles, in press). It has been suggested that failure to recognise writing on the skin is a sign of brain immaturity; this, however, is not firmly established.

(F) This is no longer true. The phenomenon is now known as 'semantic satiation'; it has been extensively studied in recent years (see, for instance, Kounios *et al.*, 2000; Black, 2001).

(G) I now recognise that I was far too incautious over my use of the word 'normal'. In view of the ambiguous overtones of the word 'abnormal', to use language which could be taken to mean that a dyslexic person is abnormal in some disparaging sense is wholly unacceptable.

(H) These 'extraneous' movements are now being studied systematically by Turner Ellis *et al.* (in preparation).

(I) The idea that there could be a failure of integration when stimuli are presented visually as well as when they are presented auditorily seems to me in retrospect to be an ingenious one. There is a limit to the speed at which auditory information can be presented. However, what I now think I should have said is that in dyslexics the speed of information processing is impaired.

(J) The important point, it now seems to me, is that if we use the dyslexia concept this gives us a different view as to the direction of causality. There may be anxious parents and a child lacking in confidence as the **consequence** of the literacy problems, the original cause being a constitutional one. I was anxious at the time to give the psychoanalytic approach fair consideration, but even in those days I regarded the ideas of Blanchard as rather far-fetched. Now that the constitutional basis of dyslexia has been established by brain-scan techniques there is even more reason to be sceptical. In the early stages of my research, of course, I had to make judgements, sometimes on quite inadequate evidence, as to what approach and what concepts would turn out to be most useful.

(K) In the 1961 paper I give a quite erroneous list of what the developmental aphasic child might find easy and difficult; in particular I suggest that they would perform well on memory items!

FINAL THOUGHTS

I now think that Brenda's difficulty in drawing the plan of her house and drawing a bicycle is atypical of dyslexics in general. Certainly I found that in later writings I had no occasion to use the expression 'constructional apraxia'. It is clear, however, that I was aware even at the time of some of the problems in determining a dyslexic child's intelligence, and this problem was one which very much came to the fore in subsequent years.

Looking back, I am now aware that there were many interesting points about Brenda's and Michael's spelling errors whose significance I did not appreciate at the time. The commonly accepted view nowadays is that dyslexics have a deficit in the area of **phonology**, that is in the recognising, remembering and ordering of speech sounds. When I wrote the original paper, this idea had not come to the fore. It was my colleague and former pupil Dr Mary Kibel who alerted me to the important distinction between spelling errors which are due to a lack of spelling knowledge and errors which are 'phonological' in the sense that they involve misrepresentation of speech sounds (Kibel and Miles, 1994). I now recognise that many of Brenda's and Michael's spelling errors are phonological, e.g. 'disdons', 'wafs' etc. Kibel (2004) points out that phonological errors are particularly likely to occur when two sounds are similar in their place and manner of articulation. In this work Kibel has made a detailed study of the conditions in which phonological errors occur.

Another concept which had not come to the fore, at least in Britain, at the time when I was writing the 1961 paper was that of **multisensory teaching**. Nowadays, when I explain this expression to parents, teachers and others, I explain that dyslexic pupils should be encouraged to look carefully, listen carefully and pay careful attention both to their mouth movements in saying the word and their hand movements in writing it. In so far as I trained Brenda and Michael to pay attention to their tongue, lip and mouth movements as they said the words, I was in a sense giving them multisensory teaching, even though I had not then heard of the word.

Overall I think it fair to say that with increased experience I have changed some of my views on points of detail but not on what I take to be the essentials. In particular I believe now, as I did then, that dyslexia is a syndrome, with the implication that it has a constitutional cause. For this reason any parental worries and any lack of confidence on the part of the child are the consequences of this limitation, not their cause.

I was wrong in thinking that the main feature in dyslexia was a visuo-spatial problem or a confusion over direction; I now believe it is a problem of dealing at speed with language and symbols. I do not believe that what I called Brenda's 'constructional apraxia' is typical of dyslexics in general, and I believe that the expressions 'mirror writing' and 'reversal' give a misleading theoretical account of situations where a child writes 'b' for 'd' or 'p' for 'q'. These, however, are points of detail and do not signal any major change of approach.

NOTES

Note 3.1   One of the referees commented: 'I think the author should make clear that this kind of thing is extremely rare.' I am thankful to say that I resisted this suggestion on the grounds that I did not know whether it was rare or not. During the next two decades I came to realise that the expression 'extremely rare' was very far from the truth!

Note 3.2   The reference here is to Kant's *Critique of Pure Reason* (1781). In the section entitled 'Transcendental Aesthetic' Kant argues that we are so made that we **necessarily** experience things as laid out in space and as occurring successively in time. Time can be thought of as a line even though we know a priori that different times are successive.

Note 3.3   Orton had offered an ingenious anatomical theory, in which he referred to 'strephosymbolia' – literally 'twisting of symbols' – to explain confusions between 'b' and 'd' ('static reversals') and the writing of letters in the wrong order ('kinetic reversals'). Part of the input from the optic chiasma goes to the left side of the brain and part to the right side. Anatomically these two inputs are mirror images of each other; thus when there appears a memory trace corresponding to a 'b' in one hemisphere there will be a memory trace corresponding to a 'd' in the other. In the case of most children the 'wrong' memory trace becomes suppressed and the letters 'b' and 'd' are read and reproduced correctly. In strephosymbolia, however, the mirrored memory trace still exerts an influence.

Orton, however, appears to have been unaware of the contribution of Gestalt psychology to this issue (see, in particular, Koffka, 1935). It was a central tenet of Gestalt psychology that the phenomena of perception could not be understood simply in terms of a 'local sign' theory – the pattern on the retina of the eye is not sufficient to explain how it is that our perceptions are **organised** – that they have a Gestalt-quality. Orton's theory of strephosymbolia seems to imply a rather simplistic acceptance of the 'local sign' theory.

4 The Word-Blind Centre

Early in 1962 I was surprised to receive a letter from Dr Alfred White Franklin, who was then chairman of the Invalid Children's Aid Association. It invited me to take part in a conference at St Bartholomew's Hospital on the theme of dyslexia or word-blindness; the invitation had arisen because he had read my paper on the subject (Miles, 1961).

Dr White Franklin held a senior post as physician at St Bartholomew's Hospital. I afterwards learned that he had been coming across a significant number of children who were refusing school and in some cases showing signs of stomach upsets and the like. I rate him as one of the unsung heroes of the dyslexia movement since he had the insight to appreciate that these school-refusers had one thing in common – **they had difficulty in learning to read and spell.**

Dr White Franklin had consulted the literature on what was then called 'word-blindness', and the purpose of the conference was to bring together those who might be interested in the manifestations in question – whatever name one might give them. It is interesting in retrospect to note that my description of Brenda and Michael in Miles (1961) must have been recognisable by him as relevant to the theme of the conference. I think it fair to say that in 1962, although there was clearly a need to be cautious in our claims, we at least had some reasonably clear idea of what we were looking for. There was, after all, a not inconsiderable literature already in existence, even though Orton's (1937) work was largely unknown in Britain and Hinshelwood's (1917) pioneering work had largely been ignored. The paper by Morgan (1896) describing a boy called Percy who wrote his name as 'Precy' and made some other strange spelling errors did not become widely known until the 1970s.

The conference was a decidedly stormy one. There was a foretaste of the heated and not always very courteous arguments which were to rage about the concept of dyslexia for the next 20 years. I remember one educationalist warning us that if we used this esoteric term 'dyslexia' we would be 'tying a ball and chain' on our teachers. I think he was somehow under the impression that if educational difficulties had a neurological basis there was nothing one could do to remediate them. When a mother complained that her child had not received suitable help, an attempt was made (in a letter written to me after the conference) to discredit her evidence by saying that she was 'a psychiatric patient'. The letter also implied that if I libelled educational authorities by implying that they were incompetent I might find myself taken to court.

My own contribution to the conference was a modest one (Miles, 1962): I simply reported on some of the techniques which I had used with Brenda and Michael. I also made a few contributions to the overall discussion.

A record of the conference proceedings still survives (White Franklin, 1962). One of the things which I particularly noticed in Dr White Franklin's foreword to this volume was his uncompromising attitude to those who were out of sympathy with the central theme of the conference and did not accept the idea of word-blindness or specific developmental dyslexia. In his foreword to the conference report he writes: 'In support they [the opponents of the concept] produced the arguments which doctors recognise as traditional among those colleagues who oppose changes or advances in the aetiology or treatment of disease in patients. One confessed to a prejudice against the idea; another had never seen a case; a third had treated a mass of children with complete success and without any need for the concept.' As will be seen in Chapters 10 to 13, controversies of this kind came very much to the fore in the next two decades.

What had clearly emerged from the conference was the existence of a need. There were parents who had struggled in vain to obtain help for their children, and it appeared that in most of Britain adequate provision was virtually non-existent.

As a follow-up to the conference Dr White Franklin invited some of us whom he knew to be sympathetic to his overall approach to form a committee. The committee members were Dr Macdonald Critchley, Professor Oliver Zangwill, Professor Patrick Meredith, Maisie Holt and myself. We were later joined by Dr Mia Kellmer Pringle, a much respected figure in the world of education. Dr Critchley was to become President of the World Federation of Neurology; Professor Zangwill, who was Professor of Psychology at Cambridge University, was sympathetic to the venture primarily, I think, because of his experiences with brain-damaged patients at the end of the second world war; the idea that there could be developmental anomalies not unlike those found in brain-damaged patients was an idea which obviously made sense to him. Professor Patrick Meredith was Professor of Psychology at the University of Leeds. Although considered by some to be rather eccentric, he was in his own way a highly imaginative and creative thinker. Maisie Holt was a psychologist who had taught dyslexic children at St Bartholomew's Hospital but was somewhat reluctant to discuss her methods.

It was service on this committee which persuaded me to make dyslexia my main research interest. There was obviously a need for people to carry out assessments, quite apart from the need for research. In response to letters addressed to the committee I carried out a small number of assessments in London at the Invalid Children's Aid Association's headquarters in Queen's Gate. Then, at some stage – I am not sure exactly when but it must have been around 1963 – I decided to carry out assessments in Bangor. This was in the newly formed Department of Psychology (Chapter 5), not, as previously, at the local Child Guidance Clinic, though I still kept up my links with the clinic by going there for about half a day a week.

Throughout my academic life I have always taken the view that academic psychologists should not lose touch with what is sometimes called the 'real world', the implied contrast being with the ivory towers of academia.

I was lucky at the time to have links with St David's College, Llandudno, where the headmaster, John Mayor, encouraged me to assess and teach boys at his school.

At this stage I had to be particularly careful not to claim too much. I made clear that I could promise no results but only that I would do my best to try to help.

My meetings with members of the Invalid Children's Aid Association committee were a constant source of stimulation. With its limited funding the Association had set up a 'centre' – it comprised two caravans – in Coram's Fields in north London, and it was here that the committee used to meet.

Quite early on we received a visit from Marion Welchman, later to become a leading figure in the dyslexia movement worldwide. One of the teachers at the centre was Gill Cotterell from whom I learned a great deal on the teaching side; and her 'Checklist of Basic Sounds' – two sides of green paper – proved a standby over many years.

The first director of the Centre was Dr Alex Bannatyne. He did not stay long, but subsequently made many valuable contributions to dyslexia work in the USA. One of my recollections of Dr Bannatyne is that he suggested to the committee that the term 'word-blind' was out of date. We did not get rid of the term altogether but compromised by re-naming the centre the 'Word-Blind Centre for Dyslexic Children'.

As director of the Centre in succession to Dr Bannatyne we were fortunate to be able to appoint Sandhya Naidoo. This appointment was a striking success, and Sandhya's book *Specific Dyslexia* (Naidoo, 1972) was the first in Britain to make systematic comparisons between recognisably dyslexic children and suitably matched controls.

It had never been Dr White Franklin's intention to keep the Word-Blind Centre going in perpetuity. I think originally he had in mind a period of about five years, but its life span turned out to be nearer nine years, though I do not remember the exact date when it eventually closed down. The Invalid Children's Aid Association, however, had primed the pump, which was the original intention: enough had been done to convince at least a minority of people that there was something here which was worth investigating. It was for others to determine how the ideas initiated at the Centre might be developed.

RECOLLECTIONS

By the mid-sixties Marion Welchman had begun her pioneering work in the dyslexia field – prompted initially by the unsympathetic treatment meted out to her son, Howard, in his early days at school. Marion had heard about the work of the committee of the Word-Blind Centre and with characteristic energy had sought us out. I first met her at one of the committee meetings, where she was received with the utmost courtesy by Dr White Franklin and Dr Critchley. However, the person who first introduced her to us described her, in a rather disdainful voice, as 'a mother from Bath who thinks she may be able to do something'. At the time, of course, none of us knew how much this mother from Bath would be able to contribute to the understanding of dyslexia not only in Britain but on a worldwide scale. From our first meeting Marion and I shared a private joke: I often referred to her as the 'mother from Bath'. The private joke was eventually made public in Hales (1994, p. vi).

I was afterwards to make many friends on the other side of the Atlantic. There was the much loved Margaret Rawson. Margaret lived from 1899 to 2001, dying at the age of 102, after spanning three centuries. Other good friends included Dr Richard Masland, who, like Dr Critchley, was at one time the President of the World Federation of Neurology, and his wife Mary (Molly) Masland. There was also Dr Sally Childs, a staunch defender of the Gillingham Stillman programme. I was also very lucky to have the opportunity of meeting with Dr Norman Geschwind, an inspirational and innovative neurologist. There was also Dr Albert Galaburda (one of the first people to carry out post-mortem examinations of the brains of those known to be dyslexic in their lifetime), Dr Drake Duane, Roger Saunders, Thomas West, Dr C. K. Leong, Dr Dwight Knox, Professor P. G. Aaron and, most recently, Dr Leonore Ganschow, a psychologist interested both in language learning and in the reading of music (see Ganschow et al., 1994). I should also like to mention Professor Ingvar Lundberg of Sweden, Dr Zdeněk Matějček of the Czech Republic, Dr Edna Freinkel of South Africa and Dr S. Ramaa of Mysore, India. On a visit to Australia I had the chance to meet Professor Gordon Stanley (who was one of the first researchers to discover dyslexics' slowness at processing symbolic information when it was presented visually, and Dr John Reddington, a former student at Bangor who moved to Australia to carry out his research in Brisbane and who masterminded the travel arrangements for Elaine and myself when we visited Australia. I have been lucky to have had such a large number of good friends from many different parts of the world.

5 A Service for the County of Gwynedd

I had not been serving for long on the Word-Blind committee when the University College of North Wales, Bangor (as it then was) decided, as part of its expansion programme, to create a Department of Psychology and to appoint a professor as its head. I applied for this post and was successful.

In those days funding came from the government via a body called the University Grants Committee. I remember shortly after my appointment that its chairman, Sir John Wolfenden, visited Bangor and made clear to the college senate that the government had no wish to dictate to universities how they should spend their money. I was fortunate to have been able to spend most of my academic life with these funding arrangements. In the 1980s, however, all this changed: universities were told to apply to industry and elsewhere for funds to support their research. The result, not surprisingly, was that criteria for what was valuable in research were determined largely by market forces and by researchers' ability to convince the appropriate committees that their proposals were of value. It is symptomatic of the changed climate that, shortly before my retirement, I was told that, in addition to being head of the Department of Psychology, I was now head of a 'Cost Centre'!

If I had had to convince the educational establishment of the time that research into dyslexia was of value, I do not think the dyslexia research at Bangor would ever have got off the ground – much of my time would have had to have been spent in making (probably unsuccessful) applications to grant-giving bodies, whose educational advisers could well have been hostile at the very mention of the word 'dyslexia'.

Fortunately, however, in the 1960s and 1970s, as head of the Psychology Department at Bangor, I was left free to investigate any topic of my own choosing without any interference from the government. My academic colleagues on the college's faculties and senate were invariably supportive, and although I continued from time to time to publish books and papers in areas other than dyslexia – particularly on the philosophy of behaviourism (Harzem and Miles, 1978) and on the philosophy of religion (Miles, 1959, 1998) – dyslexia research occupied by far the largest part of the time which I had available. As I said earlier, I was never an 'ivory tower' academic, and it seemed to me that dyslexia was an area where there might be interesting practical applications.

During my early time at Bangor I had wondered if I should make a study of juvenile delinquency. There were, however, no prisons in the immediate neighbourhood, and as my experience increased I came to realise that trying to rehabilitate offenders called for skills which I did not possess.

After my year at the Tavistock Clinic (1953–4) it was also clear to me that psychotherapy *à la* Melanie Klein was not for me either: some of Klein's ideas seemed to me very wild and speculative (compare my comments on psychoanalysis in Chapter 3). On one occasion at the Bangor Child Guidance Clinic I ventured on an interpretation of a child's feelings in terms of sexual fantasies – I asked the child tentatively, 'Was it anything to do with going to the toilet?' The result was a totally blank response; I was given no indication that my proffered interpretation of the child's feelings had in any way touched on something important in her life. I am not of course disputing that, in the right context and with the right clients or patients, people's lives can be transformed by psychoanalysis; nor am I disputing the importance in most contexts of happy human relationships. I am saying only that for purposes of understanding dyslexia the psychoanalytic approach does not seem to me the best way forward. In contrast, my experiences with dyslexic children and their parents and with dyslexic adults continually convinced me that I was on to something. For example, when I gave talks to local Dyslexia Associations and described some of the behaviours which I believed to be manifestations of dyslexia, I could tell that the audience were nodding in approval, as if to say, 'This is exactly what we have found in **our** child.'

On one occasion I had written a report which had been passed to an educational psychologist in a neighbouring county, and I received a letter – not exactly hostile but certainly exhibiting scepticism – asking what in detail were the tests which I had used. I invited her over to sit in on an assessment and explained in advance that many dyslexic teenagers had difficulty in learning their 'times tables'. The girl whom we were to test came into the room shortly afterwards, and before we had spoken for many minutes she volunteered, 'I have such difficulty in learning my tables.' I heard a gasp from my colleague who was sitting beside me; later she went on to do highly skilled work in the dyslexia field. Looking back on the episode it occurs to me that **without** the dyslexia concept as it then existed in my research – it included difficulty over learning 'times tables' – the possibility of predicting that someone would come into the room and announce that they had difficulty in learning 'times tables' would have been extremely remote. In that respect dyslexia was a powerful concept, whereas I had found no such powerful concepts either in the study of delinquency or in some other branches of psychology, such as the study of intelligence.

I continued with the methods which I had been using with Brenda and Michael (see Chapters 1 and 2). From the mid-1960s it was possible, as I indicated in Chapter 4, to form links with St David's College, Llandudno. Some of their boys used to come to Bangor for remedial teaching and sometimes assessment.

By 1970 I had sufficient confidence in what I was doing to submit for publication a small book of 70 pages (Miles, 1970). In the preface to this book I refer to some of the controversies over dyslexia and write: 'If this were a purely theoretical issue there would be little justification for heated argument. In practice, however, my experience is that when the value of the term "dyslexia" has been disputed or not recognised, the result has often been an appalling failure even to appreciate what the problems of these children are, let alone to press for adequate remedial facilities.'

I am in no doubt now, just as I was at the time, that, if dyslexic children are to be helped, an understanding of their distinctive needs is essential.

I did not believe that if children were taught to read they would necessarily learn correct spellings, but my hope was that if they were taught to spell this would thereby improve their reading.

The basic procedure was that the pupil should have a notebook (their 'dictionary') in which words were written down in families. The first page contained three-letter words (consonant, short vowel, consonant), with the words *bag, beg, big, bog* and *bug*. I had used these words with Brenda and again in the paper which I had submitted at the conference at St Bartholomew's Hospital eight years earlier (Miles, 1962). In due course the teacher could move to consonant blends – *clap, strap, step* etc. – and consonant digraphs – *sack, sock, suck* etc. The long 'a', the long 'i' and the long 'o' were then introduced, and the pupil was encouraged to listen for the difference between, say, *hat* and *hate* and told that where the vowel sound was long an 'e' had to be added. I found that, in the case of the children whom I was teaching – most of them, admittedly, were bright – the words 'consonant' and 'vowel' and the words 'long' and 'short' (applied to vowels) could be explained at quite an early stage.

Vowel digraphs were then introduced, such as 'ee', 'ea', 'oa' and 'ou'. At the appropriate time other word families could be introduced, such as *butter, gutter mutter*. I also thought that it would be helpful to show how the same root could generate different word forms, for instance *wait, waited* and *waiting*.

I remember that on one occasion I visited a school where the headmaster suddenly wrote a word on the blackboard, saying, 'Who can read this?' The word was 'POISON'. It occurred to me, therefore, that there were a few words which children in the interests of their own safety needed to read by any means open to them: the words which I chose were 'danger', 'poison', 'toilet' and 'police'.

I realised that if dyslexic children were told simply to **learn** spellings these would not be remembered for any significant length of time – at most for long enough for them to pass a spelling test and thus deceive their teacher into thinking that their spelling was better than it actually was.

At no time during the lesson did I expect the pupil to be able to spell a word unless I had shown him or her how to set about it. I might encourage them to generalise, for instance by pointing out that if they could spell *might* and *light* they could also spell *bright*, but, generalisation apart, I required them to spell only words which had the same pattern as those already in their dictionary. A few pupils had difficulty in recognising when words rhymed, but this was rare (see Miles, 1993a, Chapter 18 for some evidence from my records).

At the end of *On Helping the Dyslexic Child* (Miles, 1970) there were exercises in which the words to be spelled were chosen either to test what the pupils had been shown in the most recent lesson or to revise words which had been shown in earlier lessons. An important principle was not to give them too much to attend to at the same time. In the case of *bag, beg, big, bog* and *bug*, for instance, the 'b' and the 'g' would look after themselves, and this would leave the pupil free to concentrate on writing the correct vowel. It was in fact possible to extend this policy still further by asking the pupil simply to make a judgement of **same/different**. Thus if a child wrote 'p' for 'b' or vice versa I would say, 'bat–pat – same or different?', randomly interspersed with 'bat–bat – same or different?' My experience was that dyslexic children, though they may well write 'p' for 'b' or vice versa, could detect differences between confusable letters when these differences were pointed out to them.

It was clear by the late 1960s that requests from parents for help for their dyslexic children were on the increase. At an early stage Aline Wiggin, a retired headmistress of a primary school, joined me in the teaching. I had always gone on the principle that 'diagnosis without treatment is unethical', and when people came from a distance I always tried to put them in touch with someone in their locality who could do the teaching. Despite my training at the Tavistock Clinic I was never opposed to the idea that parents should teach their own children in the absence of suitably experienced teachers, who were very rare birds in the 1970s. On some occasions I used in a light-hearted tone of voice to present the parents with the analogy of a husband teaching his wife to drive a car. A laugh, of course, does wonders to ease feelings of stress, and I would suggest that even if parent and child fell out with each other from time to time during the lessons this was a small price to pay for helping the child to achieve literacy.

The major breakthrough came when I was joined in the work by my wife, Elaine. She was a qualified teacher who had also received special training in philology. She realised that if we were to make progress on the teaching side those who did the teaching had to be properly trained. By this time the demand for lessons was growing. Our response was to invite a number of qualified teachers – many of whom had young families and wished only for part-time work – to join our team and teach for three or four hours a week. In the early stages we used to meet at our house and exchange ideas on how best to solve a problem which had arisen in the case of a particular child. This was a very valuable opportunity for us to learn from each other.

An incidental advantage accruing from the fact that the dictionary and sentences used in *On Helping the Dyslexic Child* had a fixed structure was that if for any reason the pupil had to change to a different teacher the teacher who was handing-over the pupil could explain to their successor precisely what stage in the programme the pupil had reached, for instance, 'We have done the "ea" words but not the "ow" words.'

After a few years Elaine and I published a jointly authored book (Miles and Miles, 1975). This book was later combined with Miles (1970) to form Miles and Miles (1983a). In the two later books there was some modification to the choice of sentences for revision. In addition both books had chapters on the teaching of arithmetic – an area to which we both later devoted considerable attention (Henderson and Miles, 2001; Miles *et al.*, 2001; Miles and Miles, 2004).

Miles and Miles (1975) also had a chapter entitled 'Problems of morale', which reflected our growing awareness that our teachers should make clear that they understood the pupil's difficulties, or at least were prepared to try to understand by listening to the pupil's own account of them. It is possible for dyslexic children to undergo inner turmoil without their teachers – or even their parents – being aware of the fact.

In this connection we quoted the telling words from Sir Walter Scott's *The Pirate*: 'the most cruel wounds are those which make no outward show'.

In both the two later books there were also chapters entitled 'Word-beginnings and Word-endings'. There were suggestions for teaching handwriting; there was an account of the 'doubling' rule – that if a short vowel is followed by a consonant that consonant is usually doubled – and it was pointed out that, with a few exceptions, long vowels or pairs of vowels are followed by 'ch' and short vowels by 'tch'.

In all three of these books the pupils were asked to construct their own dictionary and were introduced in a systematic and structured way to letter–sound correspondences. The overall aim of the books was to provide common-sense guidance for those parents and teachers who recognised the existence of some kind of problem but were unsure how to proceed. We went on the principle that dyslexics were weak at memorising but strong at generalising, and we tried to create the conditions in which their ability to generalise meant that there was less to memorise.

Ann Cooke also contributed a very valuable book for teachers (Cooke, 1993, revised version 2002).

Originally, by arrangement with Dr Gareth Crompton, Chief Medical Officer of Health for Anglesey, dyslexic children from Anglesey were taken by taxi to the Psychology Department at Bangor for their lessons. On Elaine's initiative, however, it was arranged that teachers from the Dyslexia Unit (which was part of the Psychology Department) should visit the pupils in their own schools and teach them, usually separately, occasionally in pairs, in any room which the school had available. The norm was one lesson per week, although in special cases this was increased to two. When the counties were reorganised in 1974, the teaching arrangements were extended to the whole of the new county of Gwynedd.

From 1973 onwards it was possible to collaborate with the college's School of Education in providing courses on dyslexia which could form part of a Master's degree in Education or a Certificate of Further Professional Studies. Lecturers from the Department of Psychology, Education and Linguistics provided an academic background to the courses.

6 First Steps Towards Quantification

When Elaine took over responsibility for the teaching services, it left me free to concentrate on assessment. I was glad to have had some experience of teaching: I was at least in a position to be aware of some of the difficulties which our teachers would have to face. My problem was to devise an approach to assessment which could properly be called 'scientific'. As a result of my philosophical training I was aware that there are all kinds of ways of doing good science, and I knew that it was important for me not to be tied by any methodological straightjacket.

A book which profoundly influenced my thinking was Miller (1966). Here are two passages which have always seemed to me of particular interest and importance.

The first is from Chapter 6, pp. 95–6:

A great scientist, Lord Kelvin, once said, 'When you cannot measure ... your knowledge is of a meagre and unsatisfactory kind'. He was, of course, a physicist ... There is a long list of creditable sciences which do not rely on measurements ... In truth, a good case could be made that if your knowledge is meagre and unsatisfactory, the last thing in the world you should do is to make measurements. The chance is negligible that you will measure the right things accidentally.

The second passage is from Chapter 20, pp. 337–339:

For several years there has been a running battle between the clinical heirs of Sigmund Freud and the statistical heirs of Sir Francis Galton. The Freudians learn about people by talking to them; the Galtonians give tests and compute statistics. When both groups are not both busy doing this, they like to spend their time criticising each other.

Then follows a 'table of compliments', based on the controversies of the time. Here are a few examples of the plaudits and criticisms made by both sides. According to the statisticians their own method is **operational, verifiable, objective, rigorous** and **scientific**. In contrast that of the clinicians is **hazy, subjective, unscientific, uncontrolled** and **unverifiable**. The clinicians, on the other hand, say that their own method is **meaningful, rich, sensitive, true to life** and **understanding**, whereas the statistical method is, among other things, **trivial, superficial, sterile, oversimplified** and **pseudoscientific**.

I remember my mentor, Professor Oliver Zangwill, once saying to me that, before one started to research any area in psychology which had practical applications, one should talk to the practitioners, sit in on their discussions and, in general, get the feel of what the subject matter of the topic to be researched was about. This was good advice as far as dyslexia research was concerned. My first priorities were to meet parents, to talk to teachers and, above all, to gain the confidence of the children themselves so that they were willing to tell me what their difficulties were. To this day I particularly value what people tell me about dyslexia in a clinical setting, even in the absence of tables of figures (norms) which tell me how frequently this or that type of behaviour occurs.

Chapter 1 and Chapter 2 of this book each contain one statistical table: both tables compare the proportion of errors over consonants to the proportion of errors over vowels in the spellings of Brenda and Michael. This apart, I reckon that it was not until the late 1960s that I started to consider the issue of measurement, and it was not until the mid-1970s that in my dyslexia research I used any measuring apparatus more sophisticated than a stopwatch. I took heed of George Miller's warning about the risks of trying to measure anything when one is unsure of one's ground.

There was still the issue of 'clinical versus statistical' – was I to be mainly a clinician who only occasionally collected statistics, or was I to insist that at every stage of the research my conclusions should be based on sound statistical principles?

It seemed to me that in dyslexia research it is possible to have the best of both worlds. It is sometimes said that people make clinical judgements 'intuitively'. I think this means that they arrive at conclusions without being fully aware of their reasons for doing so. I do not know if women are particularly good at making such judgements, but when it is said that a wife knows 'by intuition' that her husband is tired I suspect that what may have seemed to a casual observer like some inexplicable gift of understanding is in fact the ability to make use of and combine small cues. This, at any rate, is what I think is done in a clinical judgement of dyslexia: there are small signs which, taken in conjunction, lead one to say, 'This case has a dyslexic **feel** to it.'

If this is so, it ought not to be all that difficult to specify what these small signs are. This is an issue to which I shall return when I come to discussing ways in which the Bangor Dyslexia Test (Miles, 1997) might be scored.

What was needed in an assessment for dyslexia, so I thought, was a specification of what responses should count as 'dyslexia positive' and what responses should count as 'dyslexia negative'. If enough 'dyslexia positive' responses were present, this would justify the claim that the person was dyslexic.

From the start I had not been happy with any policy of 'definition by exclusion' – by which one judged a poor reader and speller to be dyslexic if no obvious reason for their poor reading and spelling could be found. Such reasons might, for instance, be lack of intelligence or lack of opportunities for learning.

By the same token, when at a later date people started to distinguish dyslexics from 'garden variety' poor readers, I was far from happy. 'Garden variety' poor readers were in effect poor readers of low IQ. I counted up four things which I think are wrong with the expression 'garden variety poor readers'. First, it assumes that 'dyslexia' means the same as 'poor reading'; and from the very early stages I was convinced that there was much more to dyslexia than this. Secondly, it implied that dyslexics cannot be of low intelligence, and I saw no justification for this supposition. Thirdly, there were problems with the concept of IQ, as I shall make clear in Chapter 9. Fourthly, the evidence of systematic differences between dyslexics and these allegedly 'garden variety' poor readers was at best inconclusive. In the absence of reliable differences the distinction seemed to me to serve no purpose. My hope is that the expression 'garden variety poor reader' will be consigned to the scrap heap.

There are, of course, poor readers and spellers whose poor performance is the result of a lack of ability and others where there has been the lack of opportunity to learn. However, it was my view from the start that the genuine dyslexic was different, and I suspected that subtle indications of this would be available if one had the skill to read the signs correctly. This suspicion has been confirmed by the fact that some of the experienced teachers in the Bangor team have been known to say to me, 'This feels (or 'does not feel') like a genuine case of dyslexia.' The challenge was to make specific (or 'operationalise') the cues on which such a judgement might be based. It would then be possible to distinguish the genuine dyslexics from those who were poor readers or spellers for other reasons.

As part of my philosophical training I had been influenced over many years by Popper's (1963) principle of falsifiability; and I was aware from early on that if I was to research dyslexia adequately I would need to supply criteria not only for saying that a person **was** dyslexic but also criteria for saying that they were **not**. Indeed when I gave talks on dyslexia I was sometimes asked – I suspect by those with suspicious minds – whether I ever found any negative cases. I was, of course, able to offer full reassurance that I sometimes did (see Miles and Miles, 1983a, pp. 25–26).

In my quest for scientific rigour there was a further major problem. Any test, so I was always led to suppose, if it is to be credible, must have validity, that is it must measure what it purports to measure. But how was I to achieve this in a test for dyslexia? Had a suitable test already been in existence I could have validated the Bangor Dyslexia Test against it. My problem, however, was that I could find no test which measured dyslexia in the sense which I wanted to give to the word. Moreover, had such a test been in existence a further test would have been unnecessary. My procedure therefore had to be different. I do not know how far I was aware of this at the time, but I now see that what I was doing was to define dyslexia in a particular way and then see what could be done with the results.

Critchley (1970, p. 11) refers to 'a specific type of developmental dyslexia occurring in the midst of but nosologically apart from the *olla podrida* of poor readers'. By 'nosologically apart from' he is suggesting that a distinctive classificatory label is required (see Chapter 10 for further discussion of the word 'nosological'). 'Olla podrida' is a Spanish stew with mixed ingredients, and the word has come to be used for a 'miscellany of any kind'; the expression 'poor readers' covers, in his view, just such a miscellany. The concept, then, which I wished to develop was what Critchley called 'specific developmental dyslexia'. At the present time it is commonly agreed in Britain – though not to the same extent in the USA, where the influence of Samuel Orton appears to be waning – that the word 'dyslexia' should be understood to mean 'specific developmental dyslexia' in Critchley's sense.

In effect, therefore, the question which I was setting myself was: 'If one can devise a test which picks out dyslexics in the required sense, can anything interesting be done with the results?' My task was therefore to devise a test which would pick out a group of individuals who were scientifically interesting. It was not my job simply to find a 'dictionary' definition of dyslexia – a report on how people have used the word. The classifications which occur in ordinary speech are far from useless, however, and I clearly needed to come up with an operational definition which was not too far removed from the imprecise ideas of ordinary language. During my reading I came across a passage from the philosopher Sidgwick (1922, p. 264), which seemed to me to indicate what I needed. The passage ran as follows:

> A definition may be given ... which will be accepted by all competent judges as presenting, in a clear and explicit form, what they have always meant by the term, though perhaps implicitly and vaguely. In seeking such a definition we may, so to speak, clip the ragged edge of ordinary usage, but we must not make excision of any considerable portion.

There was no question, therefore, of trying to validate the Bangor Dyslexia Test against other tests for dyslexia. My task was to specify a particular view of dyslexia – or, if you prefer, to 'operationalise' such a view – and then see if anything interesting could be done with the results. In particular I would need to specify, à la Popper, what predictions could be made from this concept and explore whether those picked out as dyslexic were in any way distinctive. Clinicians such as Critchley had argued that specific dyslexia is a syndrome; if, therefore, I was able to operationalise the manifestations of this syndrome, it was possible that interesting findings might emerge.

RECOLLECTIONS

As was indicated above, I was sometimes asked if I ever found any negative cases. In this connection I should like to place on record the following episode.

It was not normally my practice to respond to what may be called 'adversarial' comments – those which, often as a result of misunderstanding, purported to be critical of the dyslexia concept. On one occasion, however, the parent of a child whom I had assessed sent me a report from a Director of Education (in an area, be it said, not very near Bangor) who wrote that they were taking no notice of my report 'because at Bangor everyone assessed there turns out to be dyslexic'. Had this been hearsay evidence I would of course have ignored it, but the words were in front of me in writing. I therefore wrote to this Director, inviting him to come to Bangor to see for himself what we did. To my surprise his deputy, who in fact had written the offending words, accepted the invitation. Little was said on his arrival about this issue; he expressed a keen interest in our work, and only as he was leaving did he say how embarrassed and sorry he was about having made the comment. We even agreed that if people were referred to an eye clinic it would hardly be surprising if many of them turned out to have eyesight problems!

7 The Bangor Dyslexia Test I

How, then, did the Bangor Dyslexia Test originate and what did I wish it to achieve? In the first place I believed that dyslexia was a syndrome – a family of manifestations, having a constitutional basis. There was in the 1970s only circumstantial evidence for the constitutional basis: the condition ran in families, which suggested a genetic basis, and, more speculatively, it was possible that there were analogies between the behaviour of the children whom I was assessing and the behaviour of adults who were known to have suffered brain damage. I was no neurologist, however, and believed that there was plenty to be found out by a systematic study of my subjects' behaviour.

As a result of reading the relevant literature, by talking to other workers in the field and above all by letting my subjects talk to me I looked for items for inclusion in my test which I thought might be part of the syndrome. Here were some of the things which I thought might be relevant.

UNCERTAINTY OVER LEFT AND RIGHT

Because it appeared that dyslexic subjects had problems over left and right, it was clearly useful to ask them in the first place if they could show me their right hand. I came to realise that slight hesitations and pauses might be significant. Soon afterwards I decided to add the supplementary question, 'Did you have any difficulty when you were younger?' This gave the subjects a chance, if they so wished, to tell me about earlier problems – perhaps, indeed, earlier reprimands – and in many cases the use of compensatory strategies. I wondered if the double command, 'Touch your right ear with your left hand' would present any extra difficulty compared with the single one.

I had learned from Head (1926) that aphasic patients had difficulty in imitating Head's hand movements as he sat opposite them: an act of symbolisation was required since the patients had to deduce that Head's left hand corresponded to their own right hand and vice versa. It seemed that there was not the same difficulty if both tester and patient faced the same way.

I became aware that, if anything useful was to be gained from tests involving left and right, several trials were required: if only a single trial is given, there is insufficient opportunity for the subject to go wrong. More importantly the task had to be made more difficult. This is why I introduced the double task, for instance: 'Point to my left eye with your right hand.' One such item might have been manageable by a dyslexic, but a succession of tasks would be more difficult, given that they involved not only working out left and right but also attending to the words 'eye', 'hand' or 'ear'.

Over the years I learned of a wide variety of strategies for remembering left and right – 'I am double-jointed in my right thumb, so if I waggle the double-jointed thumb I know it is my right'; 'I imagine myself back in school where I knew that in one classroom a particular building was on the right'; 'I wear my watch on my left wrist'. In this connection I remember a boy who deduced my left side because it was the side on which I wore my watch. In general the compensatory strategies of the intelligent dyslexic are amazingly ingenious.

From time to time I noticed that, in order to answer the question 'Which is **my** right hand?' some subjects turned in their seats. I had a gut feeling that this was part of the syndrome, but it was only later that I felt I understood why this was happening. Dyslexia is a **labelling** difficulty and in this item of the Bangor Dyslexia Test it is the **labels** 'left' and 'right' which cause the problem. One can save oneself one of the two labelling tasks by turning in one's seat so as to face the same way as the tester. Turning in one's seat is an action – something which one **does** – and the subjects who turn in their seats are in effect using an ingenious compensatory strategy by which **doing** something (turning in their seats) is a substitute for **naming**.

REPEATING POLYSYLLABLES

Among the more difficult words at the end of the Schonell Word Recognition test (Schonell and Schonell, 1952) is the word *preliminary*. What I have found with dyslexic children and adults is that responses which I had not believed were relevant to the diagnosis suddenly 'hit me in the eye' as having a significance which I had hitherto not appreciated. In this particular case I do not know how many times I had given the later part of the Schonell Word Recognition test to my subjects before I realised that stumbles over the word *preliminary* might be of diagnostic relevance. From then on I made a point of trying to notice whether such stumbling occurred. In this connection I consulted with my colleague Gill Cotterell, who had been teaching children at the Word-Blind Centre in Coram's Fields (see Chapter 4), and asked her if she had encountered anything similar. She said she had, and told me of a boy who had said 'par cark' for *car park*. Soon afterwards Elaine and I were giving lessons to three brothers who came to our house accompanied by their mother. She explained that the boys' father was also dyslexic and that, though he said that he wished to be philosophical about it, he just could not say the word *philosophical*. Into the Bangor Dyslexia Test, which I was working on at the time, went the word *philosophical*. Other words which were added were *anemone* and *statistical*.

In an earlier version of the test I included the word *competition*. After all, it was a word of four syllables – and, if memorisation of that number of syllables was the problem, therefore dyslexics would have difficulty with it. They did not, and *competition* was removed from the test. I later came to realise that it was not the number of syllables as such which was important – it was rather the problems which the subjects encountered in having to articulate the words. Thus to say the m-sound the two lips have to be touching each other, while to produce the n-sound the tongue has to be placed on the alveolar ridge. It follows that to articulate the words *preliminary* and *anemone* what is required is to move at speed between places of articulation which are very close together. The same goes for the 'ph', 'l' and 's' sounds in *philosophical*. In the case of *statistical* the most common error is to say 'satistical'; it is possible that in failing to repeat this word accurately the dyslexic child is at the same stage as some younger non-dyslexic children. It is known that a consonant cluster followed by a vowel and consonant is harder to articulate than consonant-vowel-consonant, and it therefore makes sense that the first 't' should be omitted. The second 'st' is different: because the 't' begins a new syllable (sta-tis-ti-cal, and in this position in the word the 'st' is not perceived as a cluster. The initial 'st' is also in an unstressed syllable, and phonemes in unstressed syllables are always more vulnerable than phonemes in stressed ones (note 7.1).

TIMES TABLES AND SUBTRACTION

I had been asked at one point to teach spelling to a dyslexic boy from St David's College who, I was told, also had difficulty in learning his times tables – would I help? I had no idea why the boy found his tables difficult, but I can never resist bait and therefore agreed to explore the matter. When I did so, it became immediately obvious that his difficulty with his tables was part and parcel of his dyslexia. I also noted that, although he was aged about 12, he still used his fingers for calculation.

From this point on I became aware that problems with calculation were manifestations of dyslexia. I therefore had no hesitation in including some subtraction items and the task of reciting tables in the Bangor Dyslexia Test. I suppose you could say that I was widening the concept of dyslexia so that it included these two mathematical items, but this seemed preferable to limiting the concept to 'poor reading' and then being confronted with a mass of disparate phenomena, which often accompanied poor reading. There was a need for a concept which linked these disparate phenomena together.

In the Subtraction test I chose a mixture of easy and hard items. I needed to check if my subjects could give the answer 'in one' or whether they needed to do some working out, for instance using their fingers or marks on paper or by devising a special strategy. If, for instance, you are asked what is $44 - 7$ and you know your 10-times table, as my subjects almost always did, it is possible to use $4 \times 10 = 40$ as an anchor point and count in ones to reach the correct answer. Almost all my subjects could manage the 'regular' tables – the 5-times, the 10-times and the 11-times – and there was, of course, the unfailing regularity that the numbers go up in ones. I always noted if my subjects could respond instantly, and, if they could not, I was interested not so much in whether their answers were correct but rather in the strategies which they used for arriving at them.

I was in no doubt that most of my subjects of suitable age would be able to say the 5-times, the 10-times and the 11-times tables, and I excluded the 9-times table on the grounds that a few of them might know the rule that the successive numbers of the 9-times always add up to nine (0–9, 1–8, 2–7 etc.), and it was likely that some of them would know the 2-times, 3-times and 4-times tables. This left me with the 6-, 7- and 8-times tables, which I therefore included in the test, with the option of having the 4-times table available if necessary for use with the younger children. I used to start them off by saying, 'One six is six', and their responses turned out to be fascinating.

When I came to collect control data, I was amazed to find how many of the control subjects could rattle off their tables with no hesitation. One thing in particular which I learned from my dyslexic subjects was how easily their memories became overloaded. To recite tables as required in the Bangor Dyslexia Test it is necessary both to calculate the next number (if you do not know it already) and also to keep track of where you are in the table. A common response, which I always regarded as significant and therefore scored as dyslexia-positive (see Chapter 8) was any question such as, 'Was it six sevens I was up to?', since this indicated that the subject had had too much to hold in mind.

Additionally the 'tables' item provided plenty of other opportunities for dyslexic manifestations to show themselves. I found that some subjects asked if they could just say 'Six, 12, 18', leaving out what for scoring purposes I have called the 'preamble' – 'one six is … two sixes are …' etc. I soon came to ask myself why they did this, and I am now fairly confident that it is a memory phenomenon: having to include the preamble imposes an extra load on the memory, and for a dyslexic this can sometimes be the last deciding straw which leads to a loss of place.

I noticed also that subjects would sometimes break into the 'wrong' table, as exemplified by, 'Seven sixes are 42, seven sevens are 49, eight sevens are 56', and sometimes there would be 'slips' – which were quite often corrected, for example 'eight 80s – I mean eight eights'. It was also interesting to note that, even after making a mistake, a subject might well continue with the correct algorithm. If you say, 'Three sixes are 17' it is quite logical to say, 'Four sixes are 23' – and the typical dyslexic is perfectly capable of logical reasoning.

At one point I learned that there were some children in schools who were not taught to say their tables. I therefore prefaced the Tables item in the Bangor Dyslexia Test by asking, 'Did they teach you tables at school?' If at any time the answer had been no, the subject's responses would not have been usable since many non-dyslexics would have produced seemingly 'dyslexic' responses. I do not remember a single answer of no, but this possibility had to be taken into account in the scoring and interpretation of the results. One would have had to make a decision about the presence or absence of dyslexia on the basis of nine items instead of 10.

MONTHS FORWARDS AND MONTHS REVERSED

I do not remember how exactly Months Forwards and Months Reversed came to be included. I remember finding that almost all the children whom I assessed were able to say the days of the week correctly, except in the case of the very young ones. This meant that a request to say the days of the week would not have differentiated the dyslexics from the non-dyslexics. The reason for this was also clear: in the case of the days of the week there are seven items to remember, compared with 12 in the case of the months of the year, and, since the days of the week come round more frequently than the months of the year, there is more opportunity for learning them. I decided to retain the request to say the days of the week as an option in the case of the seven- and eight-year-olds, since although a successful response would be uninformative a failure would be a highly significant positive indicator.

DIGITS FORWARDS AND DIGITS REVERSED

I routinely made use of intelligence tests (see Chapter 9 for an account of the problems which I encountered in this area). I found, however, that some of the tests, including the Terman–Merrill and the Wechsler, included items where the subject was required to recall strings of auditorily presented digits. These included both Digits Forwards and Digits Reversed. I had become aware quite early on that many dyslexic children were weak at the recall of digits; and, since one of the things which I was looking for was incongruity – poor reading or spelling in relation to intelligence – it seemed absurd to use a recall-of-digits test as a measure of intelligence; this would have the effect of making this incongruity appear less than it actually was. It would be far more useful to include a recall-of-digits item as one of my tests for dyslexia. This was therefore what I decided to do.

'b'–'d' AND OTHER CONFUSIONS

It had also been well documented by Orton (1989) that many of the children whom he examined tended to write 'b' for 'd' and vice versa. When children came to me for assessment, I made a point of asking the parents to bring school exercise books and other samples of their written work. From these I was able both to examine their spelling and check for 'b'–'d' and other confusions.

FAMILIAL INCIDENCE

It was clear that the condition which I was studying often ran in families. This, indeed, had been convincingly documented by Hinshelwood (1917) and by Hallgren (1950). It would obviously be useful, therefore, if, as part of the assessment, I could check if any other members of the family had similar problems. As will be seen, this was not an easy item to score, but any evidence which I could obtain would clearly be very important.

FINGER AGNOSIA

At one point I considered including a test for finger agnosia – one in which the subject would be blindfolded and asked to indicate which of one, two or more fingers I was touching. However, on the few occasions when I tried this nothing very exciting seemed to emerge; I therefore did not include this item as part of my routine examination.

The test therefore comprised 10 items in all – left–right, polysyllables, subtraction, tables, months forwards, months reversed, digits forwards, digits reversed, 'b'–'d' confusions and familial incidence. A version of the test containing these 10 items was published in 1982, while in the 1997 version (Miles, 1997) a small number of changes were made. In the next chapter I shall consider how responses to these items might be scored and what the results might signify.

NOTE

Note 7.1   I am grateful to my colleague Dr Michelle Aldridge who as a phonetician gave me considerable help with the 'repeating polysyllables' item.

8 The Bangor Dyslexia Test II

Combining a clinical approach with a statistical one was not always easy. At an early stage in the research I presented a paper to my colleagues with the title 'How Do I Score the "crikey?"' The situation which I envisaged was one in which a subject, presented, for instance, with a request to say the months of the year, responded, 'Oh, crikey!' – and then proceeded to say the months of the year correctly. Was I to ignore the 'crikey' on the grounds that it was a one-off remark which could not be quantified? On the other hand, if I simply ignored the 'crikey', I would clearly be throwing away useful information. I did not at the time produce any answer to this question. However, I now think that a suitable answer would be to specify that, for instance, 'any exclamation of dismay, puzzlement etc.' should be recorded and counted.

I suggested in the last chapter that clinical judgements were based on the use of a combination of cues, sometimes small ones, which required to be pieced together. This, of course, is what happens in any medical diagnosis. If I could operationalise these cues, I would be in a position to make a judgement as to whether a particular indicator of dyslexia was present or absent and quantify the numbers of each. In the event I found that I would sometimes be presented with a response which I regarded as marginal – not clearly indicative of the presence of dyslexia but also not clearly indicative of its absence. I therefore devised the following notation: a clearly dyslexia-positive response would be scored as 'plus', a marginal response as 'zero', and a dyslexia-negative response as 'minus'.

If the subject answered the question with no difficulty, hesitation or special strategy, this qualified as 'minus'. If there were hesitations and other signs of uncertainty or if the subject needed a special strategy in order to work out the answer, the response was scored as 'zero', while, if I judged a response to be typically characteristic of dyslexics, it was scored as 'plus'. When totting up the number of dyslexic indicators, I decided to score a 'zero' response as half a 'plus', which meant that two 'zeros' were equivalent to one 'plus'. If there was a single hesitation, this was regarded as insignificant, but if there were two or three hesitations this was scored as a 'zero'. One of the decisions which I had to make in scoring the test was whether there were, in conjunction, enough positive signs to be significant.

A complete list of what responses should be scored as 'plus', 'zero' and 'minus' will be found in the test manual (Miles, 1997). Examples of 'plus' responses included turning in one's seat in order to work out the tester's left and right sides, asking if the months of the year needed to be said in order, losing the place during the recitation of tables ('Was it six sevens I was up to?') and making a mistake in trying to repeat, say, five digits but repeating six correctly.

'Zero' responses included more than a single hesitation or request for the question to be repeated and 'slips' in the reciting of tables, for example by saying 'eight eighties' instead of 'eight eights'. The result was also scored as zero if the subject responded correctly but only as the result of a special compensatory strategy, for instance being able to show his or her right hand correctly because it is 'the hand I write with'. It seemed to me that hesitations over the Left–Right item might indicate a general uncertainty, not over direction, as I first thought, but over which label, 'left' or 'right', was the correct one to use. I found, incidentally, that among those who scored 'plus' on the 'Left'–'Right' item there was no excess of left-handers or of those with unusual handedness or eyedness (Miles, 1993a, Chapter 21).

Some of the responses which were scored as 'zero' were of the sort that might be thought insignificant in ordinary conversation, for example asking for the question to be repeated. It is possible that in the early stages of the research I missed their significance. Later I appreciated that if you have a memory problem you may well lose track of what has been said and ask for it to be repeated, or possibly you may try to keep track of what has been said by repeating it to yourself subvocally. A memory weakness of this kind is clearly an important diagnostic indicator.

Sometimes it seemed that hesitations indicated the need to take time to work the answer out. Similarly requests for the instruction to be repeated, subvocal rehearsal, echoing the question ('Let me see – my left hand with your right, was it?') might all indicate a failure to grasp instantly the import of the question, and this might be indicative of the dyslexic's language-processing difficulties.

If there were a sufficient number of wrong answers, the result had, of course, to be scored as 'plus'. However, what particularly interested me was not wrong answers as such but the way in which the subject arrived at the answer. This was why I had to take note of small signs such as hesitations and requests for the question to be repeated. A tick was, of course, always acceptable if the subject produced the correct answer with no hesitation, but I always discouraged test users from simply putting a cross if the answer was wrong; one needed more information about the circumstances in which the error occurred.

At an early stage of the research it was essential to try the items out on children in an ordinary classroom. There would be no point in scoring a response as 'dyslexia-positive' if I found that a large number of non-dyslexic children also made the same response. I am grateful to a former honours student of mine, Ian Pollard, for collecting data from schools in the Manchester area on most of the items which I was planning to include in the test. These were adequate spellers who on the basis of two items (Similarities and Picture Completion) from the Wechsler (1949) test were within the average range for intelligence. I was thus in a position to have some idea of what non-dyslexic children of different ages were able to achieve. Inevitably, however, there was the problem of drawing boundaries: how was I to determine what were normal limits for a non-dyslexic child? At what point should I decide that this or that response merited a 'zero' or a 'plus' as opposed to a 'minus'?

The basic requirement was to achieve the fewest possible number of false positives (non-dyslexics who came out as dyslexic) and false negatives (those who were dyslexic but were not picked up by the test). The data collected by Pollard showed me that the drawing of boundaries, though not wholly arbitrary, could not, from the nature of the case, rest on totally firm foundations.

Here are some examples. Quite a number of the children tested by Pollard made **one** error in the Subtraction items. This meant that if 'one error' was to be scored as a 'plus' or even as a 'zero' I would be opening the way for an excess of false positives – since you could make an error over subtraction without being dyslexic. On the other hand, if I required, say, four errors before scoring the result even as a 'zero', this would open the way to a large number of false negatives – those who were dyslexic but were not picked up. In the last resort I had simply to plump for what I judged to be the optimum place in which to draw the boundaries and trust to there being enough redundancy in the test for users to be able to avoid serious misclassification. In this particular case I decided that two errors in the Subtraction items should count as a 'zero' and three errors as a 'plus'.

I found that the ability to repeat polysyllables correctly increased with age. The scoring therefore had to take account of this, with the result that three words not repeated accurately counted as 'plus' at age 10 and over, whereas at age 15 and over only two failures were needed.

It was at this point that I was able to bring in Popper's (1963) principle of falsifiability. The children whom I had been seeing were, in my view, showing the manifestations of dyslexia, but what would be the predicted results if I was wrong? I would find that among normal spellers of average intelligence there would be as many dyslexia-positive responses as there were among those whom I judged to be dyslexic. This could be put to the test with minimal trouble and expense by giving the Bangor Dyslexia Test to these other children as a control group.

As a result of a shortage of resources it was possible to make comparisons only on seven out of the 10 items in the Bangor Dyslexia Test – checking school books for 'b'–'d' confusion and arranging to meet families to discover about familial incidence would have been very time-consuming, and, as a time saver, the Digits Forwards subtest was omitted. Full results have been published in the test manual (Miles, 1997) and in Miles (1993a, Chapter 7).

It was possible to collect data for 132 controls. In what follows I have included a table which originally appeared in Miles (1993a, p. 56). It relates to 80 dyslexics and 80 controls between the ages of nine and 12.

The dyslexics in this age range were found to have a mean number of 'pluses' (out of a possible seven) of 5.14, standard deviation 1.20, while the controls had a mean of 2.24, standard deviation 1.37. Statistically this difference was highly significant (note 8.1). With regard to the individual items, the percentage of dyslexics and controls showing 'pluses' is given in Table 8.1.

This meant that my attempt to falsify my hypothesis had been unsuccessful. The items in the Bangor Dyslexia Test were differentiating those whom I had judged to be dyslexic from normal achievers. Had this result not been obtained, my whole enterprise would have been broken-backed.

What in fact I found was not that non-dyslexics **never** produced the specified responses or that dyslexics **always** did so. It was rather that, overall, dyslexics were more vulnerable. It also appeared to be the case that items which were difficult for

Table 8.1. Percentage of dyslexics and controls, aged nine to 12 years, who scored positive on seven different items from the Bangor Dyslexia Test

Item	Dyslexics	Controls
Left-Right	78	42
Polysyllables	56	24
Subtraction	58	19
Tables	96	51
Months Forwards	60	13
Months Reversed	86	28
Digits Reversed	80	48

Adapted from Miles (1993a)

non-dyslexics would be extra difficult for dyslexics and items which were easy for non-dyslexics would be not easy but at any rate less difficult for dyslexics.

By taking the relative percentages of dyslexic and control children who scored 'plus' on the various items it was possible to make judgements about the diagnostic value of these items. Thus 96% of the dyslexics came out as positive on the tables item compared with 51% of the controls. In contrast, only 13% of the controls failed to recite the months of the year correctly, compared with 60% for the dyslexics. Thus a 'minus' on tables would be a strong counter-indicator of dyslexia, while a 'plus' on months of the year would be a strong positive indicator.

Two final points require discussion. The first is that on the Bangor Dyslexia Test, as in most other tests, correct responses can be learned. The second is to point out how the Bangor Dyslexia Test gives subjects the opportunity to go wrong.

With regard to the first point, what I have come to realise is that, for the most part, the correct answers to items in the Bangor Dyslexia Test are not taught in school. In particular it is no part of the syllabus to train children to distinguish 'left' and 'right' – it is something which the majority just pick up. Nor is practice normally given in repeating polysyllables, saying the months of the year or repeating strings of digits. It was a revealing experience when I assessed a boy who had nine 'pluses' out of 10 on the Bangor Dyslexia Test and was successful only in repeating the months of the year correctly. When I mentioned to his mother that I was surprised, in view of his other difficulties, at his success with this item, she gave a wry smile and said: 'We have spent ages and ages learning them.'

I see no reason why in principle it should not be possible for a child to learn correct responses to any item in the Bangor Dyslexia Test, and if this happened on any large scale some different items would be needed or greater weight would have to be attached to reports of earlier difficulties and the use of compensatory strategies. It is no accident that the Bangor Dyslexia Test does not include tests of reading and spelling, since these are taught in schools and the variety which I encountered, particularly in the case of scores on the Schonell Word Recognition test (Schonell and Schonell, 1952), could be attributed to environmental factors – the quality of the teaching received and the opportunities for learning available – more than on the constitutional factors in which I was interested. The children whom I assessed were mostly poor readers and spellers in spite of the opportunities which they had received.

In the case of the Left–Right items and the Subtraction items 'special strategies' were allowed for in the scoring, while the reciting of the harder tables (6x, 7x, and 8x) and the confusing of 'b' and 'd' show up dyslexic limitations in spite of there having been opportunities for learning. Familial Incidence is the one item in the 10 where opportunity for learning can play no part at all.

With regard to the second point, I have come to realise that dyslexia is a disjunctive concept – it can show itself by either this manifestation or that, or rather by specified manifestations in a given case (as it might be, manifestations a, b, d, f and h, and in another case by manifestations b, c, d, f and k). This is why I have never been happy to say that any one item in the Bangor Dyslexia Test is a decisive indicator of dyslexia; a diagnosis is reached by considering the pattern as a whole. A 'plus' or 'zero' response here or there may be of no special significance, but if there are several such responses one starts to wonder if they are merely coincidental, and with increasing numbers of positive indicators the hypothesis that the person is not dyslexic becomes increasingly difficult to maintain.

In the 10 items between them there is arguably enough redundancy to compensate for the fact that in a given case some of them may not be usable for diagnostic purposes, for example the Tables item in the case of children who had never been taught their tables or the 'months of the year' item in the case of a child who had been systematically taught them. In general the Bangor Dyslexia Test took the form it did because of the culture in which it originated, and it determines the form which dyslexia takes in that particular culture. Dyslexia needs a particular culture in which to manifest itself, but as the culture varies so will the manifestations.

I have never been willing to place emphasis on the precise number of positive indicators found on the Bangor Dyslexia Test by a given individual. I am not prepared to say that someone with six 'pluses' is 'more dyslexic' than someone else with five. What I do say is that in our particular culture to give someone the Bangor Dyslexia Test provides them with the opportunity to display dyslexic manifestations. Not all the manifestations will be present in any one individual, and there exist many opportunities other than those supplied by the Bangor Dyslexia Test for individuals to manifest their dyslexia (note 8.2).

NOTES

Note 8.1 $t = 14.50$, $p < 0.001$.

Note 8.2   In its present form the Bangor Dyslexia Test lacks any measure of an individual's ability to process symbolic information at speed. A research project to remedy this deficiency is urgently needed.

9 Assessing Intelligence

The question of how to assess a dyslexic's intelligence is discussed in Miles (1996) in a paper entitled 'Do dyslexic children have IQs?' In it I express scepticism about the value of the concept of IQ in general and suggest that there are particular problems in the case of dyslexics.

The idea that an IQ figure represents a fixed quantity and therefore implies a limit as to what a person might achieve seems to me a pernicious doctrine when applied to any individual, and particularly pernicious when applied to dyslexics. I have been influenced on this matter by my reading of Skinner (see Harzem and Miles, 1978, especially Chapter 7). Skinner and his followers have shown the many things which can be achieved by creating appropriate conditions in the environment.

The possibility of providing a global IQ has been taken for granted even by those whose main aim has been to break down cognitive skills into their components. Such researchers report in meticulous detail on their subjects' ability to read non-words, to make lexical decisions ('Is this a word or not?') and to break words down into their separate phonemes, yet in some cases they uncritically cite IQ figures (obtained, one suspects, by someone else), without any consideration of the sub-skills of which the IQ figure is composed. The central problem is that if one tries to assess the intelligence of dyslexics by using the traditional intelligence tests to produce a global IQ figure, one finds that some of the items tap not the strengths of dyslexics but their weaknesses.

In the Wechsler test there is the notorious ACID profile: this is a shorthand for saying that dyslexics are weak at four specified items, symbolised by the letters A, C, I and D – Arithmetic, Coding, Information and Digit span. In Miles and Ellis (1981, p. 230) there is a discussion of why some dyslexics might be weak at some or all of these four items. For instance, there is an item in the Arithmetic subtest which requires a knowledge of 'times tables', and this is likely to be hard for dyslexics, however intelligent they may be in other ways. For some items there is a time limit, and a subject who exceeds this limit is adjudged to have failed. In another case the item may be repeated – something which may well be necessary for dyslexics because of their poor immediate memory – but no extra allowance of time is given. The Coding subtest requires the processing of symbolic material at speed, and dyslexics are notoriously weak at this. The reason or reasons for a relatively low score on the Information subtest are not fully clear, but it seems likely that the dyslexic's poor performance is an indirect, rather than a direct, consequence of their dyslexia – because there are many things going on in their environment it could be that, because of their dyslexia, dyslexics miss out on some of them and therefore have less general knowledge. That dyslexics tend to have a low span when digits are presented auditorily is well established. Later versions of the Wechsler test make this item optional.

The Terman–Merrill (1960) test also contains 'digit span' items. It also contains 'memory for sentences' items, and it is established (Miles *et al.*, in press) that many dyslexic adults are weak at this. I have also put on record (Miles, 2004a, p. 8) the fact that in some items of the Terman–Merrill test some of my subjects were able to solve the apparently 'difficult' part of the item but failed to pass it as a whole because of a lack of elementary numeric facts, for instance that $4 + 9 = 13$ or $18 + 9 = 27$. Similarly many of my subjects were able to respond correctly to the series of Direction items in the Terman–Merrill test (as it might be, 'Which way would you have to face so that your right hand would be towards the west?') only if they could draw a diagram of the points of the compass – but the instructions lay down that the subject may not use pencil and paper.

In a study by Thomson (1982) dyslexics in three different age bands (8.0 to 10.11, 11.0 to 13.11 and 14.0 to 16.1) were tested on the British Ability Scales (Elliott *et al.*, 1983; an earlier version of this battery of tests was published in 1979). Compared with the test norms they were consistently weak at Speed of Information Processing, Immediate and Delayed Visual Recall, Recall of Digits and at Arithmetic. They were above average, however, at Formal Operational Thinking, Similarities, Matrices, Block Design and Word Definitions. Thomson's study confirms yet again the unevenness of the profiles of dyslexic children on different subtests, while also showing the risk of underestimating their strengths if one provided a global IQ figure contributed to by both their strengths and their weaknesses. Because someone has laid down that certain specified responses to items in traditional intelligence tests shall be deemed to be indicators of intelligence, it does not follow that such 'deeming' is justified.

I shall be returning to Thomson's study in Chapter 19. In the British Births Cohort Study the measure which we used to assess intelligence was the combined score on the British Ability Scales Similarities and Matrices tests.

There is not the same difficulty with the Raven Matrices tests. They demand the ability to recognise patterns and relationships but require little by way of memorisation or counting. I, in fact, regularly used the Advanced Matrices (Raven, 1965) with subjects over the age of 16 whom I believed to be bright. Some of them obtained scores which were well above the norms (mean 21, standard deviation 3) given by Raven for university students (Miles, 1993a, Chapter 31).

The type of reasoning in the Raven Matrices tests is similar to that described many years earlier by Spearman (1927). Spearman distinguishes between two types of reasoning ability – that of educing correlates and that of educing relations. Thus, if we consider the test item 'Here is to there as now is to ...', the person being tested has to educe the relation between 'here' and 'there' and then produce the correlate term 'then'. It is, I suspect, the kind of reasoning at which many dyslexics would excel.

My general problem was that if I did not obey the instructions in the test manual to the letter I would be departing from standardised procedure and any resultant IQ figure would be invalid; or I could follow the standardised procedure at the cost of providing what on clinical grounds was an underestimation of the subject's reasoning ability.

My solution was this. From the Wechsler (1949, 1974) tests (WISC and, later, WISC-R) I selected the Similarities, Vocabulary, Comprehension, Block Design, Object Assembly and Picture Completion items. These items were specified in advance. Similarly I specified in advance certain items from the Terman–Merrill test – Vocabulary, Similarities, Ingenuity, Direction, Abstract Words and Enclosed Boxes. From these items I derived what I called a 'selected IQ', that is one based on selected items. I made a rough estimate that a selected IQ was about 10 to 15 points lower than a full-scale IQ; I then graded my subjects with intelligence grades of Z, Y, X, W, V and U for inclusion in the Summary Chart in Miles (1993a). Table 9.1 gives the approximate equivalents between grades U to Z and the selected IQ as determined by the Wechsler or Terman–Merrill tests and the score on the Advanced Matrices (Raven, 1965).

Table 9.1. Table of equivalences between selected IQ figures on the Wechsler and Terman–Merrill tests, scores on the Advanced Raven Matrices, and grades of intelligence from U to Z

Selected IQ	Advanced Matrices score	Grade
140 or above	26 or above	Z
130–139	22–25	Y
120–129	17–21	X
110–119		W
100–109		V
90–99		U

Adapted from Miles (1993a)

These grades represented a rank order. Also it was possible to use this set of equivalences to provide an approximate match for intelligence of dyslexics and controls when I compared their performances on the Bangor Dyslexia Test (see Miles, 1993a, Chapter 7).

My avoidance of labelling the grades A, B etc. was deliberate – I did not wish to imply that someone who came out as grade U was any less meritorious than someone who came out as grade Z (note 9.1).

I was also interested in recording the two highest test or subtest items at which the subject had obtained passes, for instance two passes at the first grade of Superior Adult on the Terman–Merrill test or scaled scores of 15 and 16 on the Wechsler Similarities and Object Assembly items. I was able to show my subjects (and their parents, if I was assessing children) these high scores, which I hope they found encouraging.

Overall, then, without committing myself to the controversial concept of a global IQ or any idea that there was a limit on what a dyslexic person might achieve, I was able to quantify my subjects' intelligence and establish that lack of reasoning power could not have been a causal factor in creating my subjects' literacy problems.

NOTE

Note 9.1   At one point I contributed a paper to a philosophical journal in which I pointed out that intelligence was a concept that was highly value-laden, and I called attention to the use of the word 'superior', which occurs in both the WISC and the Terman–Merrill tests. Those who reported that certain ethnic groups in the USA were of lower intelligence were, whether consciously or not, making value judgements and not simply reporting facts (see Miles, 1976).

Part II The Struggle for Recognition

Part II The Struggle

10 PRO and ANTI the Dyslexia Concept: A Dialogue

In the 1960s and early 1970s dyslexia was a relatively unfamiliar concept. That it should have met with opposition is not surprising; many new ideas require time before they register in the public consciousness. What was remarkable, however, was the heat which discussions of dyslexia sometimes engendered. To quote some words which I wrote at the time (Miles, 1967, p. 242): 'Whatever else we know or do not know about dyslexia, it appears to be the case that discussion of the subject makes some people extremely heated and argumentative.'

One of my reactions at the time was to try to clarify my own thinking on the controversies. As a result I decided to write a dialogue. To bring out the contrast between what I took to be opposing views I named the participants in this dialogue PRO, who was for the dyslexia concept, and ANTI, who was opposed to it.

In what follows I have reproduced some extracts, edited and occasionally modified, from what I wrote at the time (Miles, 1971).

PRO starts the dialogue by describing the typical manifestations of dyslexia and ANTI then replies:

> ANTI: Yes, of course I have met such children. But this does not mean you are entitled to say that they suffer from 'dyslexia'. If I understand correctly what may be called the 'natural' meaning of the word 'dyslexia', to say that a person is suffering from dyslexia is to say something about what is going on in the person's brain.

PRO admits in reply that he has not directly examined anyone's brain and is content to make a diagnosis of dyslexia on the basis of the person's behaviour.

> PRO: If the behaviours already described are present to any appreciable extent, I would immediately say that the child is dyslexic. By this I mean both that these behaviours are present and that the origin of the person's difficulties is constitutional.

> ANTI: I myself would never call a child 'dyslexic' precisely because, although I meet the behaviours in question from time to time, I do not know what causes them. Let me try to press my objection further. For the last eight years or so you people have been shouting the word 'dyslexia' from the housetops. Clearly you are out to promote a 'cause'; you want to get people to take dyslexia seriously, and you are saying by implication that traditional educational psychology has somehow failed in this respect. In brief, you want the term to contain 'bite'. Now it seems to me you have two choices: either you must say that dyslexia is a nosological entity, or you must limit yourself to saying that it is a nosographic one. (A footnote then explains: 'The term "nosographic" disease entity refers to a description of a particular disease in terms, for example, of its symptoms and course. The nosological entity is based on knowledge of the

cause ... Pulmonary tuberculosis is a nosological entity, since the specific factor ... the tubercle bacillus, is known.' From Hermann, 1959, pp. 94 and 101).

ANTI: In other words, either you want to make a claim about aetiology or you don't. Your dilemma, as I see it, is this. If you use 'dyslexia' as a nosological term, you are saying, in effect, that 'This person is dyslexic' entails both that he or she exhibits some of the behaviours mentioned and that these are due to some constitutional cause. If you say this, however, you are going beyond the evidence. If, on the other hand, you simply say that 'dyslexia' is a nosographic term, then you are no longer saying anything with 'bite'; your apparent victory in 'establishing the existence' of dyslexia has been obtained by definitional sleight of hand. 'All right,' I reply, 'we call these people "dyslexic" – so what?' Any claim to have discovered something which traditional educational psychologists have ignored or overlooked is sheer presumption. No wonder some educational psychologists are cross with you; they have every right to be: you are using a highfalutin term to describe what we all know about and you are implying that they have overlooked something and do not know their job. In addition, since to many people you will seem to be making a claim about causation as well, you are introducing gratuitous confusion.

PRO: I am glad you have mentioned the emotional reactions which the term 'dyslexia' has aroused in some quarters, and I think I see where the difficulty lies for some educational psychologists. In practice there have been parents who, rightly or wrongly, have been so sure that their child is dyslexic that they have had no patience with those educational psychologists who have hesitated to apply the label; they have gone for help outside the state system. With regard to telling parents that their child is dyslexic, certainly in my experience the relief to both parents and child is often quite stupendous. But let us be clear what is involved. The effect of telling parents that their child is dyslexic is logically secondary to the issue of whether the child is dyslexic. What you and I are discussing is the classificatory justification for the term 'dyslexia'; if it is not justified for classification purposes, then the fact that use of it comforts some people is of no more theoretical interest than the fact that it might conceivably be a money-winner. In the present climate of opinion, many educational psychologists attribute such failure to poor teaching or excessive parental pressure, and it is on this issue that believers in dyslexia take a different line ... If the difficulties encountered by dyslexic children were the result of poor teaching, one would expect to find groups of dyslexic children from the same class, which clearly one doesn't. As for parental pressure, if you send the parents away thinking you believe them to be neurotic worriers, this seems to me to constitute downright mishandling.

ANTI: Surely we should not be quoting cases of mishandling against one another? If a worker in the child guidance field has loaded a parent with more guilt feelings than that parent can stand, this is clearly bad child guidance. But you wouldn't like it if I blamed you for all the mistakes which believers in dyslexia have made.

PRO: Yes, of course, we all make mistakes. What I am talking about, however, is not mistakes as such but the logical implications of a technical term. We need the technical term 'dyslexia' in order to emphasise that the cause of the dyslexic person's difficulties is constitutional in origin. This explanation is radically different from explanations in terms of parental neuroticism, emotional disturbance etc., which have been put forward by many workers in child guidance clinics in the past. The reason why the label 'dyslexia' contains 'bite' is that it constitutes a challenge to some of the more conventional child guidance attitudes. In the case of these particular children, the traditional approach by which one argues from 'This child is a poor reader' to 'This child must be emotionally disturbed' is mistaken ... I am dismayed by the arrogance and lack of charity which I sometimes find when I read reports on children whom I regard as clearly dyslexic, e.g. 'His mother is a very anxious woman' or 'There appear to be a number of family tensions'. It seems to me arrogant to assume the right to pry uninvited into family affairs and uncharitable to come up – sometimes, I suspect, on very slender evidence – with such hostile comments ... My use of the term 'dyslexia' contains 'bite' in that those whose initial reaction is to try to explain the behaviours in terms of poor teaching or emotional disturbance are being asked to think again.

(Adapted from Miles, 1971)

Inevitably PRO is given the last word, and I think, in retrospect, that he could have made his points somewhat less aggressively.

However, the anger on the part of those in the PRO-dyslexia camp was not without justification. Failure to understand the dyslexia concept led sometimes to downright mishandling. I have never liked being involved in confrontation, whether on academic or any other matters. However, there were some issues over which I had to come off the fence and not just remain academically neutral.

What particularly saddened me was that ignorance about dyslexia resulted not only in failure to meet dyslexic children's needs but in hurtful accusations that they were 'not trying' and hurtful criticism of their parents. Examples of unsympathetic handling have been documented in Miles (1993a, Chapter 22), and I am reluctant to dwell on them in this book, since I hope they are now a thing of the past. For the record, however, I will cite two examples of what seem to me appallingly bad practice. The first was supplied to me by Elaine, my wife.

A psychologist wrote in one of his reports, 'This mother is neurotic.' His reason: the boy at age 11 had a reading age of nine years. The psychologist took the view that this did not constitute a very serious degree of retardation in a boy of average ability, though how the mother could be expected to know this is not clear. His conclusion was that the mother was inventing the problems and was therefore neurotic. In fact, the boy's spelling was virtually non-existent, so that he could not do the required written work, but the psychologist had made no attempt to test the boy's spelling. Recent reflection has made me increasingly conscious of the contrast between this psychologist and the wise Dr Simmons, who was the psychiatrist at the Child Guidance Clinic in 1949 (see Chapter 1), who said that he found no signs of emotional disturbance in Brenda but believed she suffered from a form of aphasia.

Secondly, I myself assessed a boy (I will call him Terence) at the age of seven years 10 months. He turned out to be typically dyslexic (case no. 7 in the Summary Chart in Miles, 1993a, and mentioned on p. 175. There is also a description of him in Miles, 1993b, pp. 96–97). One of his older sisters was clearly dyslexic (case no. 110) and another marginally so (case no. 259, who is Fiona in Chapter 21 of this book). His mother showed me a letter addressed to Terence from his senior remedial teacher. It ran: 'You have fallen behind in your reading and spelling. Let us be quite clear about this, Terence: there is no reason at all (his underlining) why you should not catch up if you make the effort ... You should learn five words each day and you should make special note of those words which you find difficult...'

To say that Terence had 'fallen behind' and that there was 'no reason at all' why he should not catch up with his classmates shows a complete failure to appreciate what Terence's difficulties were.

The accusation of lack of effort is hard to square with his own account of himself, which I discovered in one of his school exercise books. He had apparently been asked to write down what he would ask for if he had three wishes. This is what he wrote:

My thee wisces
1. I wisce that I god haF a stamp awden to geeq (changed to 'keeq') my stamps in
   I wish that I could have a stamp album to keep my stamps in
2. I wisce That I gode hepe the reFyoujes to Find homes For Them
   I wish that I could help the refugees to find homes for them
3. I wisce That I was a powem riter and bese OF all I wiisce that I gode rede
   I wish that I was a poem writer and, best of all, I wish that I could read.

Confronted by these two cases and many similar ones, I had no option but to become a campaigner and not simply an academic who did research. I was a member of the British Dyslexia Association since its inception in 1972, and I have subsequently served on the Advisory Board of the International Dyslexia Association based in the USA. Membership of these two bodies has greatly increased my understanding of dyslexia.

11 Concerns and Disputes I

One of the most cogent of the academic arguments against the dyslexia concept was that of Davis and Cashdan (1963). The authors of this paper argue that if a concept such as dyslexia is to be justified it is necessary to show that the members of this group are distinctive in respect of causation, methods of treatment and prognosis. The authors did not claim that these conditions would never be satisfied but only that at the time of writing this had not happened.

At the time Davis and Cashdan had a strong case. Certainly there was the fact that dyslexia ran in families, which suggested that a genetic factor might be at work. However, the evidence for a different brain organisation in dyslexia was only circumstantial, being based partly on the existence of possible analogies between its manifestations and those of acquired aphasia; there had been no direct examination of individual brain structures.

As things are now, of course, while there is much which remains to be discovered within the broad dyslexia framework, it would be very hard to dispute that the main causal factors in dyslexia are constitutional rather than environmental. This is why the dyslexia concept has forced us to revise our views on the direction of causality. In the past it was easy to assume that if a parent displayed worry about their child's poor showing at literacy skills, or if the child were manifesting a severe lack of confidence, the parental worry or the child's lack of confidence were themselves causal factors in producing the literacy problems. If, however, one believes that the origins of the literacy problems are constitutional, the parental worry and the child's lack of confidence need to be seen as the consequence and not the cause of the literacy problems. Parents blame themselves if they are allowed to believe that they have provided their child with an inappropriate environment, but there are no rational grounds for blaming themselves if the child's difficulties are constitutional in origin.

Davis and Cashdan are also right in saying that, at the time, there was no consensus as to methods of teaching. Multisensory methods had not come to the fore in Britain, and it was not until the 1970s that the Gillingham and Stillman (1956) programme became at all widely known in Britain. The 1970s also saw the publication in Britain of two programmes that were considerably influenced by that of Gillingham and Stillman – those of Hornsby and Shear (1975) and Hickey. (The essentials of the Hickey method will now be found in Augur and Briggs, 1992.)

I think it is now agreed that systematic teaching of letter–sound correspondences in a multisensory way is essential in all English-speaking parts of the world if dyslexics are to learn to read and spell. If one fails to provide such teaching in the case of non-dyslexics this may not be a serious obstacle to progress, but in the case of dyslexics there may, indeed, be some limited success in reading, but success in spelling is likely to be minimal (see also the discussion in Chapter 12 on 'real books').

At this point it is perhaps appropriate to record my experiences with the Initial Teaching Alphabet (ITA). This was a writing system in which there was a one-to-one correspondence between letters and sounds. On the face of it, therefore, such a writing system might seem helpful to dyslexics since it provided them with what we would now call a 'transparent' orthography – one in which each symbol consistently stood for the same sound.

Some of those whom I assessed had been taught by this method (Miles, 1993a pp. 62–63), but their parents' reactions to it were uniformly unfavourable. What happened, of course, was that the children had to learn a large number of new symbols – those of the ITA script – and then, after a short period with ITA, change back to traditional orthography. This meant that, having made the effort involved in learning to associate sounds with these new symbols – a task which dyslexic children in particular will assuredly find very hard – the children had to learn the ordinary, less regular, letter–sound correspondences of traditional orthography. In my view teaching by means of the ITA was not a good use of time.

I remember at a later date suggesting to Asher Cashdan that we knew how to teach dyslexics – that they needed to be taught letter–sound correspondences in a systematic, multisensory way. He replied, 'I agree with the method but query whether there is just one group of children for whom it is appropriate.' I agree that there remains a problem of where exactly one should draw the boundary between those who are and are not dyslexic. I am not sure if there is a continuum here or whether there are degrees of dyslexia – certainly there are degrees to which those with dyslexia are impeded by it. My own experience of dyslexics arose largely from the fact that parents sought me out, and the result was that I met mostly the more severe cases. I have some sympathy, however, at least in retrospect, with those educational psychologists of the 1970s who in the course of their work met many kinds of children with many kinds of different problems.

It is also understandable that these psychologists assumed – as did most other people at the time – that 'dyslexia' meant the same as 'poor reading'. On this premise it seems to me entirely valid to argue that the word 'dyslexia' is unnecessary: it involves the use of a highfalutin technical term for describing the obvious. Use of the word may even create the illusion that the poor reading is somehow being explained. As critics were not slow to point out, however, in this context the word 'dyslexia' explains nothing: to say, 'She is a poor reader because she is dyslexic' means no more than that 'she is a poor reader because she is a poor reader'.

Of course, once it is recognised that the word 'dyslexia' stands for a syndrome, the argument no longer holds. It makes good sense to claim that there is a link between one manifestation of the syndrome and others: one is either assigning a constitutional cause for the poor reading or one is indicating what other manifestations of the syndrome can be expected, such as phonological deficits or poor memory span.

As for the alleged lack of agreement over prognosis, it is now arguable that the prognosis for dyslexics is different because dyslexics are deviant in the acquisition of literacy skills, not just delayed. If dyslexics were merely delayed, they would perform no differently on tasks adjudged to be relevant to dyslexia from younger children matched for reading or spelling age. Many such tasks have now been used, and there is now a mass of evidence which is incompatible with the hypothesis of delay.

Nicolson and Fawcett (1995) compared the performance of 12-year-old dyslexics on a variety of tasks with that of eight-year-old controls matched for reading age. On some tasks the two groups performed no differently, but on the following tasks the eight-year-old controls performed better than the 12-year-old dyslexics. These tasks were letter naming, segmentation, non-word reading, threading beads and finding rhymes.

I, along with various colleagues, have been involved in research which appears to support the hypothesis of deviance as opposed to delay. Thus when dyslexics aged about $12\frac{1}{2}$ were asked to name visually presented arrays of five, six and seven digits, they needed more time than younger controls matched for spelling age (Ellis and Miles, 1977).

In another study reported in the same paper (Ellis and Miles, 1977) it was found that, if five digits were exposed tachistoscopically, the typical undergraduate required between 100 and 200 milliseconds' exposure time in order to reproduce them correctly. However, four highly intelligent dyslexic students, who had achieved admission to university at a time when this was a very difficult thing to do, required on average 450 milliseconds.

In a further study (Baddeley et al., 1982) 15 dyslexic boys aged nearly 13 years were compared with 15 younger children, who were normal achievers, of the same reading age. It was found that the dyslexics took longer than the reading age controls to read aloud two lists of words and non-words. In another study Wickson (1993) compared the spellings on the Schonell S1 test of the dyslexic subjects described in Miles (1993a) mean age 12 years seven months (s.d. 30.9 months) with those of younger non-dyslexic children from his own school matched for spelling age; their mean age was nine years three months (s.d. 17.9 months). He found that there was no significant difference between the groups on most of the types of spelling error classified in Miles (1993a, Chapter 9); however, in the case of errors classed by Miles as 'MOS' (misrepresentation of the sound) there were fewer such errors among the controls despite their younger age. These MOS errors are what we would now call 'phonological' errors a concept which had not come to the fore in my thinking when the first edition of *Dyslexia: The Pattern of Difficulties* was published in 1983. Wickson's study suggests that in the case of phonological errors dyslexics are deviant rather than delayed. This makes good sense in the light of dyslexics' overall phonological difficulties.

Further evidence for deviance as opposed to delay has been provided by Kibel (2004). Using a specially made 'Phoneme Coding Test' Mary Kibel compared the scores of dyslexics with those of controls of the same spelling level and with those of controls having the same scores on the Phoneme Coding Test. Compared with the controls matched for spelling level, the dyslexics took longer to resolve cluster reduction errors (1 to $1\frac{1}{2}$ years) and longer still to resolve vowel and consonant errors

(2 to $2\frac{1}{2}$ years). In the case of the controls matched for scores on the Phoneme Coding Test there were again differences – the dyslexics having particular problems when feature contrast was less, that is where there were only small differences in the place and manner of articulation of particular consonants and vowels. In an earlier study Kibel and Miles (1994) found that dyslexic children, with spelling ages ranging from 7.4 years to 11.3 years, were still continuing to make phonological errors when younger children matched for spelling age had grown out of them.

In view of all this evidence it may be concluded that the delay theory of dyslexia is very hard to defend. It follows that the prognosis for dyslexics is different from that for non-dyslexics.

We may conclude, therefore, that in the case of dyslexics there is now agreement that the cause is constitutional, that without structured multisensory teaching their progress in achieving literacy is likely to be very slow, and that because they are deviant rather than delayed there is a different prognosis for them. However, it is still arguable that Davis and Cashdan (1963) have made a valuable contribution to theory. By specifying what would be necessary for the syndrome of dyslexia to exist they have thereby provided a criterion in terms of which the existence of any syndrome can be determined. Is what people called the Gerstmann syndrome a genuine syndrome? What about dyspraxia? What about dyscalculia? Here is no place to discuss these matters, but it seems to me that this paper can make a contribution towards solving them.

RECOLLECTIONS

Most of my experiences when I spoke to local Dyslexia Associations were very positive. The following, however, is an example of the heat which discussions of dyslexia sometimes engendered. I had been indicating the need for systematic teaching of letter–sound correspondences, and on one occasion this received a frosty reception: an unsympathetic critic said in the presence of the whole audience, 'Does Professor Miles not realise that the methods which he is advocating went out of date in the 1930s?'

On another occasion a member of the audience recommended more discipline, including use of the cane. I am totally opposed to caning, and it is not an issue about which there can be much profitable argument. However, I was saved from replying by an elderly man who said: 'I experienced all the difficulties described by Professor Miles and was caned for them.' Someone then asked if the caning had done him any good, and he replied, 'None whatever.' This reply seemed to me far more telling than anything I could have said myself.

I have many happy memories both of Kathleen Hickey and of Jean Augur. Kathleen Hickey was one of the pioneers in the dyslexia field. Having been a very experienced remedial teacher she went to America to learn about the Gillingham–Stillman programme, and wrote her own programme with that as a model. When I first met her, she worked for the North Surrey Dyslexia Association, which was the forerunner of the Dyslexia Institute. Kathleen was partially disabled: she could walk short distances with the aid of a stick but often used a wheelchair. I remember a large-sized hall somewhere near London – I do not remember exactly where – in which she propelled herself from one group of dyslexic children to another. The children loved her – not least, I suspect, because, like them, she was struggling against a disability.

Kathleen was adamant that her methods were not 'phonic' – what people called the 'phonic' method was simply the 'look-and-say' method, only with smaller units. There is possibly some ambiguity here over the precise meaning of the word *phonics*. To some teachers *phonics* implied teaching children that *ker-ah-ter* spelled *cat*, which it doesn't – one needs to be very careful to clip the schwa-sound. Kathleen's method was, of course, multisensory and was much more sophisticated than that.

Jean Augur, her pupil, also taught for the Dyslexia Institute and later became education officer for the British Dyslexia Association. There was dyslexia in her family, and I learned a great deal from her sensitive understanding of the dyslexic's problems.

Another memory is of something relayed to me by a headmaster's wife who had been using the Hickey materials with a rather shy dyslexic boy, aged about 13. These materials include cards, with on one side the letter combination to be learned and on the other a written word which used the combination and a picture of whatever the word represented. The pupil has to look at the first side, make the sound which is represented and then turn the card over and read the word, with the picture as an aid. On this occasion the sound to be taught was that represented by the consonant digraph 'ff', with a picture of a cuff and the written word *cuff* on the other side. The boy duly made the 'ff'-sound and then turned the card over. In a shy voice he said to the headmaster's wife, 'That's a naughty word.'

12 Concerns and Disputes II

In the last chapter I discussed the academic arguments for and against the dyslexia concept. In this chapter I shall consider other arguments and attempt to remove some misunderstandings.

THE NEED FOR GOOD LITERATURE

There was a feeling around the 1970s that many children's reading books were dull and that it would be far better if they were exposed to 'real books', or, in other words, good literature. An extreme form of this view was put forward by Goodman (1967), who describes reading as a psycholinguistic guessing game. The overall thinking behind this kind of view was that it was unnecessary and time-consuming to try to make sense of a text by looking at every letter: children should be encouraged to use contextual information and to enjoy the book's literary style.

The concern that children should not miss out on good literature was a well-intentioned one, and arguably the use of reading books whose aim was to train up phonic awareness may at the time (though this is no longer true, see note 12.1) have led to a rather restricted vocabulary and, as a consequence, to dull reading. However, we may justifiably criticise those policymakers who laid it down that letter–sound correspondences should not be taught at all: while it may be true that fluent readers can pick up the sense of a passage without looking at every detail, this policy proved disastrous for those who were not fluent readers – and for dyslexics in particular.

I always doubted whether any of those who were against the teaching of letter–sound correspondences had ever tried to teach a dyslexic child on a one-to-one basis. In the case of children for whom learning to read is a real struggle, books which are a sufficient intellectual challenge to them may contain words which are too difficult for them to decode, whereas easy phonics-based reading books will have a better chance of giving them a taste of success. It is good sense that dyslexic children should be encouraged to make a clear distinction between books aimed at helping them to decode print and books which are up to their intellectual level. I have in my time apologised to intelligent dyslexic children who were struggling with their reading, making it clear that I did not suppose that reading about cats on mats was up to their intellectual level and explaining that the reading and spelling of easy words was necessary before they could advance to harder ones.

My own experience with dyslexics suggested to me that, as far as reading is concerned, some may have achieved limited success without the systematic teaching of letter–sound correspondences. The idea, however, that after reading 'good books' dyslexics will come to learn letter–sound correspondences and hence learn to spell seems to me very wide of the mark. Without careful and systematic teaching it is very unlikely that they would ever acquire sufficient knowledge to enable them to learn to spell accurately. If spelling is neglected in the early stages, this means that it falls to some other teacher to try to make up the deficiency when the child is older. Quite apart from the frustration which children may feel at their inability to spell, failure to teach spelling alongside reading is an uneconomical use of resources. In contrast if letter–sound correspondences are taught in a multisensory way, the child will be learning to read in the course of learning to spell.

I do not think anyone would now dispute that dyslexics throughout the world need to be exposed to good literature. It is sad, however, when their decoding difficulties make it hard for them to read this literature with enjoyment; adequate decoding skills are necessary if dyslexics are to read good books to themselves. In the meantime, while decoding skills are being learned, there is no reason why parents and others should not read good literature aloud to dyslexic children and, indeed, to any children who may wish to listen. There is no age limit at which this has to stop.

THE NEED FOR EVEN-HANDEDNESS

When resources are scarce, it goes without saying that these resources should go to those who need them most. The worry for some educationalists was that, if the dyslexia concept were accepted, resources might be channelled into helping those articulate middle-class parents who made a fuss at the expense of children whose needs might be greater. This was a perfectly valid concern. Sadly, however, things turned sour. The valid concern for a fair distribution of resources degenerated into a slanging match: politically motivated people began to sneer that this new and fashionable label, 'dyslexia', was being used by the middle classes to disguise the fact of their children's low intellectual ability. In the words of one critic: 'If you live in Acacia Avenue, you are dyslexic; if you live in Gasworks Terrace, you are thick.' Such comments were hardly likely to help the situation, and, not surprisingly, some of us found them very exasperating. This was particularly the case for those of us at the Bangor Unit who had aimed at providing a dyslexia service for **all** children in the Gwynedd area. In this we were in full agreement with the county authorities, who sent us children from every sort of background.

Fortunately it was possible to counteract the sneer about dyslexia being a middle-class invention by citing statistics from the British Births Cohort Study (see Chapters 19 and 20). These will be reported in Chapter 20. On the basis of this evidence it is to be hoped that the sneer that 'dyslexia' is a fashionable word used by middle-class parents to cover up their children's lack of intelligence will be permanently laid to rest.

MEDICAL OR EDUCATIONAL?

I now pass to issues where there were apparent conflicts but where these were due not so much to disagreement as to misunderstanding. In particular there was the issue of whether dyslexia was a medical matter or an educational one.

In the 1970s this distinction was sharper than it is now. Medical budgets were separate from educational ones and funding had to come either from one budget or from the other. From this point of view dyslexia was an awkward hybrid: no one had ruled whether it properly belonged in education or in medicine.

One of the reasons why some people objected to the dyslexia concept was because of its allegedly 'medical' overtones. In medicine it is common to use the words 'patient', 'diagnosis', 'treatment' and 'cure'; but, if a child has a reading problem, so some people supposed, such terms are inappropriate. In the words of one critic (I do not remember the source), the term dyslexia 'wraps in medical mystery what should be an educational problem'.

It is admittedly difficult to think of dyslexic children who are receiving special tuition for their dyslexia as 'patients', and although 'cure' would be appropriate if all manifestations of the dyslexia disappeared, this does not happen in practice. However, there are plenty of treatments other than medical ones, and, as for the word 'diagnosis', diagnosing is something which teachers do most days of their working lives, for example if a girl in their class is being inattentive, and the teacher attributes this to the fact that she went to bed late the previous night, it is surely quite proper to call this a 'diagnosis'.

Interprofessional rivalries may have influenced this aspect of the debate. I think that psychologists in the 1960s and 1970s, because they were not medically trained, were sometimes overly keen to emphasise how they were superior to medical doctors in their knowledge of statistics and research methods. For instance, I remember one of them writing very scathingly about 'the unsubstantiated guesses of neurologists'.

I also remember on one occasion speaking to an educational psychologist who told me that a boy's funding might be jeopardised if I described him as dyslexic and that the psychiatrist who had made the same diagnosis had no business to do so. This is a broad generalisation, to which there were many exceptions. By and large, however, I found medical doctors to be more receptive to the idea of dyslexia than were educational psychologists, and, when I asked an experienced medical doctor why this was so, he replied, 'We spend our lives looking at symptoms and it therefore comes very naturally to us to ask what these symptoms mean and what others may be expected.'

One hopes that these interprofessional rivalries are now a thing of the past. If, however, there remains any conflict in this area, it seems to me that the best way of resolving it is to say that dyslexia is a medical matter in its origin and an educational matter in its remediation. However, the whole dispute seems to be rather trivial.

'ONE SHOULD NOT LABEL CHILDREN'

I have always thought that there is an easy answer to this objection. It is that if one does not give accurate labels, such as 'dyslexic', inaccurate ones will take their place.

For example, if a teacher does not use the label 'dyslexic', other labels such as 'lazy' or 'lacking in concentration' will take their place. I remember an occasion – I had been addressing a local Dyslexia Association – when someone raised the objection about labelling. In reply a mother immediately stood up and said, 'My son prefers the label "dyslexic" to the label "dumbo".' This was greeted with prolonged applause.

'PROPONENTS OF DYSLEXIA DO NOT AGREE AMONG THEMSELVES'

Another point sometimes urged by critics of the dyslexia concept was that even among its supporters there was no agreement as to what dyslexia was. This never troubled me, since it was clearly untrue. For the record, however, it is worth pointing out that in the early 1970s Elaine and I held a meeting with Beve Hornsby (co-author of Hornsby and Shear, 1975) and Harry Chasty, of the Dyslexia Institute, to see if we could agree on some basic principles of teaching. We had no difficulty in reaching agreement: there needed to be systematic teaching of letter–sound correspondences and the teaching needed to be systematic, structured and multisensory. Dyslexia was not the controversial concept which some of its critics had assumed.

As a result of this meeting and from my visits to other dyslexia organisations I was confident that there was broad agreement between ourselves at Bangor and the various other bodies in Britain concerned with dyslexia – the British Dyslexia Association, the Dyslexia Institute, the Helen Arkell Centre, the Hornsby Centre and others – as to what dyslexia was. Those organisations, including the Dyslexia Unit at Bangor, who now run courses for the training of teachers may sometimes have differences of emphasis, which is all to the good, but there is no disagreement over fundamentals.

'ONE CANNOT REPAIR DAMAGED BRAINS'

According to this view to label children as 'dyslexic' is defeatist and discourages efforts to try to help them. The implicit argument seems to have been that if the necessary brain structures are not there any learning which requires such structures will be impossible.

Those who take this view can be reassured that that is not what advocates of the dyslexia concept were implying: there is nothing defeatist about labelling a person 'dyslexic'. Indeed, one of the main points of the label is to make sure that they **do** receive help.

It can also be pointed out that the brain is a very plastic organ which can adapt in all sorts of ways. Some people may have misled themselves by supposing it to be like a telephone exchange, where, if a wire is broken, no connection can be made. It is possible, indeed, that successful training in literacy skills itself has a modifying effect on the brain.

One could also point out that there are large numbers of constitutionally caused deficiencies which can be successfully treated. For instance, the biochemical abnormality phenylketonuria, which would otherwise lead to mental handicap, can be treated by means of a suitable diet.

In sum, the objections to the dyslexia concept were many and varied. Some were more deserving of respect than others, and in some cases nothing more was needed than the removal of misunderstandings by improved communication.

NOTE

Note 12.1   In this connection I should like in particular to mention the Lifeboats series published by Ravenswood Press. These combine interesting material with a systematic teaching of letter–sound correspondences.

13 Legislation and Governmental Recognition

The first attempt in Britain to achieve legal recognition for dyslexic individuals was in 1970, when the Chronically Sick and Disabled Persons Act of that year included a reference to 'acute dyslexia'. The word 'acute' appears to have been poorly chosen, since this word is normally taken to mean 'coming on suddenly'. In this context, however, it should presumably be taken simply to mean 'severe'. Because of this clause the Tizard Committee was appointed to look further into what was needed. Unfortunately the Tizard Report (1972) was a great disappointment as far as the recognition of dyslexia was concerned:

> We are highly sceptical of the view that a syndrome of developmental dyslexia with a specific underlying cause and specific symptoms has been identified ... We think it would be better to adopt a more usefully descriptive term, 'specific reading difficulties', to describe the problems of the small group of children whose reading (and perhaps writing, spelling and number) are significantly below the standards which their abilities in other spheres would lead one to expect.

The authors of the Tizard Report failed to take seriously the possibility that the difficulties which they described might be constitutional in origin. As a result the Report did nothing to counter the then prevalent view that literacy problems were caused by unsatisfactory relationships within the family. Also it is strange that they were willing to include references to 'writing, spelling and number' but nevertheless to recommend that we speak only of specific **reading** retardation. Sadly the opportunity to explain that dyslexia involved much more than poor reading was lost.

The Bullock Report (1975) also contained some references to dyslexia, but these were not very helpful. We were told, both in the main text (p. 268) and in the glossary (p. 587) that the term 'dyslexia' 'is not susceptible to precise operational definition'. Even at the time this seemed an unnecessarily provocative statement, and no attempt was made to give reasons in support.

I was, however, grateful to the Tizard Committee for making clear that many of the children whom they described were in need of specialist help; this enabled me in my reports at the time to say that I believed X 'to be dyslexic in the sense intended in the Disabled Persons Act, 1970, and to need special help as recommended in the Tizard Report, 1972'.

It was left to the Warnock Report (1978) to provide the machinery via which the needs of dyslexic children could be recognised and met. Until that time children with special needs had been classified according to their category of handicap – blind, deaf, having speech defects etc. Dyslexia was not one of the specified handicaps, and the best one could do by way of securing financial help for dyslexics was to classify some of them as having a different handicap, usually by saying – as was true in a number of cases – that they had a speech defect. The Warnock Report did away with these 'categories of handicap' and replaced them by the concept of 'special educational needs'. It was reckoned that 20% of the school population would have such needs at some stage in their school career, and this was a greater proportion than was receiving help at the time, and would therefore require more funds. This proposal did away at one stroke with any arguments about dyslexia: the typical dyslexic child clearly had 'special needs', and the machinery was in place for making provision for them.

In retrospect the whole idea of 'categories of handicap' seems problematic. In some cases, certainly, children could be said to have one particular handicap; in other cases, however, there were overlapping handicaps. In the last two decades there has been greater recognition of dyspraxia (clumsy child syndrome) and of ADHD (attention deficit hyperactivity disorder). In some cases there is co-morbidity with dyslexia; in some cases not. We owe to the Warnock Report a wider public recognition that children cannot always be fitted into pre-specified categories; there are all kinds of overlap.

When the Warnock Report was followed by appropriate legislation, things really started to move. The climax came in 1987, when Robert Dunn, Parliamentary Under Secretary for Education and Science, announced in the House of Commons:

> The Government recognise dyslexia and recognise the importance to the educational progress of dyslexic children, their long-term welfare and successful function in adult life that they should have their needs identified at an early stage. (*Hansard*, 13 July, 1987, 950)

This announcement marked the formal recognition of dyslexia by the British government.

RECOLLECTIONS

The non-confrontational attitude shown by Asher Cashdan (see Chapter 11) contrasted particularly favourably with that of an HMI (Her Majesty's Inspector), who was also a member of the Warnock Committee on Special Educational Needs. It was he who assured me in the 1970s that the government would **never** be willing to adopt the view of dyslexia that I myself had been putting forward. It says a great deal for the wisdom of Baroness Warnock that she was able to persuade her whole committee to support the recommendations in the Warnock Report while avoiding the current controversies about the existence and nature of dyslexia.

Over 30 years after the 1970 Chronically Sick and Disabled Persons Act had been published I attended a meeting organised by the British Dyslexia Association, at which I met Lord Alfred Morris, one of the politicians who had played a leading part in having the word 'dyslexia' included in the 1970 Act. On this occasion he told me that at the time of the initial legislation one of his parliamentary colleagues had told him that he had put on the statute book a condition which did not exist. To this he had replied, 'In that case I shall not have to spend money making provision for it.'

Part III Research and Theory

14 Further Quantification I

It was not until the mid-1970s that I began to use any experimental apparatus more sophisticated than a stopwatch. For very short time intervals, however, a stopwatch was not sufficiently accurate. I had always resisted the idea that in order to do good science one should fill one's laboratory with expensive apparatus – it was of far greater importance to decide what were the interesting questions to ask. However, at this stage of my research I took the view that there were some questions which could be satisfactorily answered only if it were possible to measure relatively short time intervals.

It had already become plain that dyslexics were weak at recalling auditorily presented digits. During the 1970s it occurred to me to ask if they were also weak at recalling them when the digits were presented visually. The presentation of stimulus material by computer was not an option at the time, and it was necessary to use a device called a tachistoscope, by means of which it was possible in controlled conditions of illumination to expose visual stimuli for time intervals as short as a single millisecond (that is, one thousandth of a second).

I started, therefore, when circumstances permitted, to present digits tachistoscopically to the children who came to me for assessment. At the same time my colleague Ian Pollard presented arrays of six digits to normal spellers aged between eight and 12 years. To ensure comparability both within my own results and between my results and those of Pollard I introduced a measure which I called the 'comparison ratio'. It represented a kind of extrapolation, from the data available, as to how many digits a subject might be able to recall in 1000 milliseconds (one second). (For further details see Miles, 1993a, pp. 135–6.) The comparison ratios for the control children in Pollard's study were found to be between six and seven digits per second, whereas the corresponding figures for those whom I myself had assessed as dyslexic ranged from 3.0 to 5.3 digits per second.

Elaine and I had long been suspicious of the idea that there were 'visual dyslexics' who learned better if material was presented auditorily, and 'auditory dyslexics' who learned better when material was presented visually. Now all the subjects in Miles (1993a) had been tested on their recall of auditorily presented digits, and data were available on 42 of them who had also been tested in the visual condition. If it were true that some subjects were visual learners and some were auditory learners, this predicts that those who scored highly in the visual condition would obtain a lower score in the auditory condition and vice versa. I divided the subjects into those who scored high, medium, low and very low in the visual condition and similarly in the case of the auditory condition. (For further details of how the groupings were obtained see Miles, 1993a, pp. 136–137.) The results are set out in Table 14.1.

Table 14.1. Comparison of grades of responding in conditions of auditory and visual presentation

		Auditory presentation			
		High	Medium	Low	Very low
Visual presentation	High	0	1	1	1
	Medium	0	1	3	6
	Low	3	5	7	3
	Very low	0	2	8	1

Adapted from Miles (1993a)

It is plain from this table that there is no clustering of results which might show that those who are strong in conditions of auditory presentation are weak in conditions of visual presentation or vice versa. There is therefore no support in these data for the view that it is appropriate to distinguish 'auditory dyslexics' from 'visual dyslexics'. Most of the subjects were, in fact, weak at the recall of digits regardless of whether the presentation was auditory or visual.

I continued to use the tachistoscope in presenting digits for short time intervals, and there are a number of other sets of experiments which I should like to mention.

In the first place another colleague, Tim Wheeler, and I (Miles and Wheeler, 1977) tested out nine dyslexics, age range 14 to 21, and nine controls of varying ages (selected on grounds of availability), in order to discover the time needed to respond correctly to arrays of five and six digits. We scored the results in terms of the number of 'bits of information' which each subject could transmit per unit of time (note 14.1). The scores of the dyslexics ranged from 11.99 to 45.10 bits of information per second, while the scores for the controls ranged from 55.92 to 93.22 bits per second. If we describe the results in terms of the subjects' ability to process information at speed, it is plain that the dyslexics were less efficient than the controls. This experiment was one of the very few in my research where there was no overlap between the scores of dyslexics and those of controls.

Since, however, dyslexia appeared to be primarily a difficulty in the processing of **symbols**, we wondered if dyslexics would be slower than non-dyslexics in tasks where no symbolisation was involved. I owe this study to the initiative of my colleague Professor Nick Ellis (see Ellis and Miles, 1978). What he did was to adapt for use with dyslexics a procedure which had been devised independently by a psychologist named Posner. In our experiment the subjects were dyslexic and control children aged between 10 and 15 years. The stimuli were pairs of letters of the alphabet. The task was to press one key if the members of the pair were 'the same' and to press another key if they were 'different'. Sometimes the stimuli were two upper-case letters, for example 'OO', 'RR' (same) or 'OB', 'RM' (different); this was termed the 'visual match' condition. Sometimes, however, a capital letter was placed alongside a lower-case letter, for instance 'Bb', 'Mm' (same) or 'Ba', 'Mb' (different); this was referred to as the 'name match' condition. It was found that in the 'visual match' condition the dyslexic subjects were not significantly slower than the matched controls in making the decision but that they were consistently slower in the 'name match' condition. The order of magnitude was not all that great (between a tenth and a fifth of a second), but it held up consistently.

One further study will be reported which involved use of the tachistoscope. It had been suggested by some researchers that dyslexics were simply **delayed** in acquiring reading and other skills. Many of us, however, believed that dyslexia was a **deficiency** – a specific handicap which would not rectify itself as the child grew older.

Ellis and I put this matter to the test by comparing 15 dyslexics, average age 12, with 15 non-dyslexics matched for spelling age, their average chronological age being eight and a half. All the subjects were presented with cards containing arrays of four, five, six and seven digits, which were presented at exposure times ranging from 400 to 1600 milliseconds. The results are set out in Table 14.2.

The comparison ratios for the control children in Pollard's study were found to be between six and seven digits per second, whereas the corresponding figures for those whom I had assessed as dyslexic ranged from 3.00 to 5.3 digits per second. On the basis of these extrapolations I argued that dyslexics could pick up fewer visually presented digits per unit of time. This result not only gave us further confirmation that dyslexics needed more time than non-dyslexics to respond correctly to visually presented digits; the fact that they were slower than younger controls matched for spelling age was evidence that dyslexics were not simply delayed but were displaying a deficit.

Table 14.2. Mean number of visually presented digits recalled by dyslexic subjects and spelling-age-matched controls at different exposure times at different time intervals

DPC = digits per card
ET = exposure time in milliseconds
Dys. = mean time in milliseconds for correct responses by dyslexics
Cont. = mean time in milliseconds for correct responses by controls

DPC	ET	Dys.	Cont.
5	400	3.44	4.37
5	800	3.95	4.87
6	400	3.88	4.97
6	800	3.94	5.24
6	1200	4.18	5.65
7	400	3.64	5.00
7	1600	4.64	6.27

Adapted from Ellis and Miles (1977)

NOTE

Note 14.1   A branch of mathematics called 'information theory' had become popular among psychologists of the time, and we decided to use information theory in our scoring. If someone indicates which of two equi-probable alternatives is the case, this is said to amount to **one bit of information**. ('Bit' is here short for 'binary digit'.) The scale used is binary, involving the successive powers of two (2^2 is 4, 2^3 is 8, 2^4 is 16 etc.). Since, counting the zero, there are 10 single-figure digits, a correctly named digit conveys 3.2 bits of information. Thus if five digits are reported correctly this represents 16 bits of information, and if six digits are correctly reported this represents 19.2 bits.

15 Further Quantification II

In this chapter I shall report some further studies, most of them carried out since the 1980s, and many of them in collaboration with colleagues (note 15.1). All relate to aspects of dyslexia, though within this broad area they are somewhat miscellaneous in character.

DO PEOPLE REMAIN DYSLEXIC?

Twenty-two of my subjects came back to the Bangor Unit for reassessment (Miles, 1993a, Chapter 19). It was therefore possible to compare the number of positive indicators obtained on the Bangor Dyslexia Test at the first assessment with that obtained at the second. My belief had always been that dyslexia is a lifelong condition, and I should have been seriously worried if I had found any large difference in respect of 'pluses' (positive indicators) between the two assessments. The scoring system of the test allows for development in the case of three out of the 10 items, Repeating Polysyllabic Words, Digits Forwards and Digits Reversed. It is assumed that even those with dyslexia will to some extent improve their performance on these three items without ceasing to be dyslexic. In the case of the other seven items adjustments for age in the scoring system were unnecessary. Clearly familial incidence does not change and if there is a history of left–right or 'b'–'d' confusion, it is possible to score a 'plus' or 'zero' on these two items, even though the manifestations of confusion are no longer present. My concern was that if there had been serious fluctuation in the number of 'pluses' on re-testing this would be evidence that the Bangor Dyslexia Test was failing to show that dyslexia is a lifelong condition.

In fact all 22 of those re-tested still satisfied the criteria for being dyslexic. Table 15.1 shows the extent to which there was fluctuation ('+' indicates more 'pluses' on re-testing; '−' indicates fewer).

It will be seen that in one of the 22 cases there was a discrepancy of three and in another a discrepancy of two. (A subject with five 'pluses' on the first testing might in principle have had any number of 'pluses' on the second testing within the range 0 to 10.) It is not, of course, in dispute that dyslexics can learn new skills and compensatory strategies, but it appears that the dyslexia itself, as measured by the Bangor Dyslexia Test, does not go away.

PERFORMANCE OF DYSLEXICS AND NON-DYSLEXICS ON THE RORSCHACH INK BLOT TEST

Ann Williams was a very experienced clinical psychologist whose home was in North America but whose family had had connections with Wales. She therefore

Table 15.1. Frequency distribution of differences in
dyslexia index between first and second assessments

Difference	Frequency
+2	1
+1.5	1
+1	–
+0.5	3
0	3
−0.5	2
−1	4
−1.5	3
−2	4
−2.5	–
−3	1

Adapted from Miles (1993a)

came over to Bangor to study for her Ph.D. This was in the 1970s. At this stage we felt we knew a certain amount about the cognitive deficiencies of dyslexics, but we certainly knew very little about them on the personality side. It seemed, therefore, that it would be worth while to ask, 'What effect does being dyslexic have on someone's personality?'

During my time with the Tavistock Clinic (1953–54) I had been taught how to use the Rorschach ink blot test, and this was an area in which Ann had received very thorough training. (The standard textbook on the Rorschach test is Klopfer and Kelley, 1943). We decided, therefore, that she should give the Rorschach ink blot test to some of the children whom I had assessed as dyslexic and that she should go out to schools in order to test controls. During a winter vacation it was also possible for her to return to New York, where she was able to test further children.

In the Rorschach test the subject is presented successively with 10 cards. The cards are not pictures of anything specific, but subjects are told that different people see different things in them and are then asked to report what they themselves can see. After several responses have been given to each card the tester, at his or her discretion, passes on to the next card. On the first run-through the tester needs to be careful not to suggest any particular response. When the subject has seen all 10 cards, the tester returns to the first card and tries to find out – again avoiding any direct suggestion – what it was about the card which made the subject respond in that particular way. This was called the 'inquiry' stage. Finally the tester goes through the cards yet again, with no restriction on direct questioning ('testing the limits' stage).

The Rorschach test has a complicated method of scoring. The tester records whether the subject was influenced by the shape of the blot, its colour (five of the 10 cards have colour on them), its texture, the presence of responses indicating movement and the presence of responses indicating activity by humans or by animals. The test is not much used nowadays and doubts have been cast on the validity of its

Table 15.2. Total numbers of responses by dyslexic and control subjects to the Rorschach ink blot cards

Dyslexics	Controls
10, 12, 10, 10, 15, 10, 10, 10, 9, 11, 5, 10, 10, 11, 10	13, 23, 14, 23, 18, 26, 14, 17, 19, 20, 24, 19

Adapted from Williams and Miles (1985)

predictions, which in the hands of some testers seemed rather speculative. However, there is nothing methodologically unacceptable about presenting subjects with ambiguous or unstructured stimuli and recording their responses.

The subjects were 15 dyslexic children between the ages of eight and 16, and 12 suitably matched controls. We were fairly confident that we could recognise dyslexics clinically, but at the time the Bangor Dyslexia Test was not yet in its final form. It had been checked that all the subjects were of no lower than average in intelligence. As a safeguard each subject was given the test on two separate occasions, several months apart, but the differences between the results on first and second testings were small enough to be ignored.

The results of the study surprised Ann. As an experienced clinician she could recognise the presence of psychosis and of organic brain damage, but with the dyslexic children there was no evidence of either. Yet their responses were very different from those of the non-dyslexic controls.

The main finding was that the dyslexics totally failed to exploit the many possibilities offered by the cards. They responded primarily to their shape, rather than to their colour or texture; they very seldom turned the cards round to get a different view of them and they gave many fewer responses overall. Table 15.2 gives the total number of responses by each child; Table 15.3 gives the percentage of 'form' responses (that is responses influenced only by the form or shape of the blot), while Tables 15.4 and 15.5 show (in two different analyses) the number of card turnings. (For confidence levels see note 15.2).

Failure to exploit the possibilities of the cards was clearly not due to any lack of intelligence. Yet the typical dyslexic in the study gave only one response per card and was influenced only by the card's shape. It is as though they were saying to the tester, 'It's a bat – and that is all I am prepared to tell you about it.'

Two explanations have suggested themselves. The first is that the dyslexics deliberately chose to keep their responses simple because of feelings of uncertainty in any

Table 15.3. Percentages of 'form' responses by dyslexic and control subjects to the Rorschach ink blot cards

Dyslexics	Controls
80, 66, 90, 90, 67, 50, 60, 70, 60, 54, 100, 100, 90, 55, 70	60, 53, 52, 30, 25, 42, 14, 35, 50, 50, 94

Adapted from Williams and Miles (1985)

Table 15.4. Number of card turnings by dyslexic and control subjects

Dyslexics	Controls
0, 1, 0, 0, 0, 1, 1, 0, 0, 0, 0, 0, 0, 0, 0	11, 3, 4, 10, 5, 10, 6, 7, 0, 10, 8, 4

Adapted from Williams and Miles (1985)

Table 15.5. Total numbers of dyslexics and controls who did and did not turn the cards on at least one occasion

Group	Turned card at least once	Did not turn card
Dyslexics	3	12
Controls	11	1

Adapted from Williams and Miles (1985)

situation which threatened to become complex. Their experience was that whenever they 'let themselves go' they were at risk of slipping up and incurring someone's displeasure. In the rather unusual social situation in which they found themselves, that is having to respond to a stranger who presented them with cards having patterns drawn on them, since a single response was socially acceptable it was wisest not to risk anything more complex. This was the explanation originally favoured by Ann Williams and myself. More recently, however, I have come round to a view which now seems to me to make better sense in the light of what is known about the cognitive limitations of dyslexics. It is that thinking up names of objects requires effort – to say that an ink blot looks like a bat or a map of Africa makes a significant demand on a dyslexic's cognitive resources, and giving only a single response involves a considerable saving of effort.

I do not know if either of these explanations is correct, but I have found that Ann Williams' findings have regularly provided an interesting discussion point for my students.

THE EFFECTS OF DYSLEXIA-CENTRED TEACHING

Dr Beve Hornsby spent a year in Bangor in the late 1970s, during which time she collected data for inclusion in a thesis for the degree of M.Ed. She had kept careful records of the reading and spelling performance of children referred to the Dyslexia Clinic at St Bartholomew's Hospital. Records were also available from the Dyslexia Institute in Staines and from our own unit in Bangor.

Beve and I set to work to check how successful the teaching had been at these three centres. What had been attempted had been not just remedial reading and spelling but the use of techniques which took into account the special difficulties of the dyslexic. The teachers had been trained to use techniques that were structured, sequential, cumulative, thorough and multisensory (note 15.3).

I had long been interested in 'single case' methodology (note 15.4). What is involved here is to see what will happen in 'baseline' conditions, that is without any intervention at all. Then comes a period of intervention, and it is possible to compare the subjects' baseline performance with their performance after intervention.

We were able to obtain measures of reading age and spelling age at the start of intervention. We then assumed, in accordance with standard practice, that children can start to have reading ages and spelling ages at age five. Then, if intervention was started at, say, age 10 on a child with a reading age of seven, the pre-teaching baseline score for reading would be $\frac{2}{5}$ (7 – 5 divided by 10 – 5), and in the same way a baseline score could be calculated for spelling. Reading and spelling ages could be taken again after so many months' intervention and the pre-teaching rate of gain could be compared with the during-teaching rate of gain. The average period over which teaching took place was about 20 months, mostly with once-weekly lessons.

We had data on over 100 children. The average rate of reading-age gain during teaching was 27.5 months, with the same figure for spelling-age gain. In contrast, when the children had been left to the vagaries of the ordinary classroom situation they had made only a gain of six months per year in reading age and only about three months per year in spelling age (note 15.5). If 'keeping up with the clock' is defined as making one year's gain in reading or spelling age per year, 85% of readers and 85% of spellers kept up with the clock. These figures show that, in general, if dyslexic children receive the right kind of help, considerable improvement in their reading and spelling is possible. Should such improvement fail to occur, it seems to me important to find out why.

The signs of dyslexia have recently become so clear that we do not now have to wait for a child to fail to read and spell before dyslexia can be diagnosed (see Hornsby, 1989). Games such as 'I spy' can be introduced at a much younger age.

STARTING TEACHING AT AGE SEVEN

Shortly before 1983 Elaine and I were given some money by the Department of Education and Science (DES), as it then was, to investigate what would happen if we started teaching the dyslexic pupils in Gwynedd at age seven instead of at age eight. We already had data on children who had started their specialist teaching at age eight, and we had obtained reasonably successful results. The question which we wanted to answer was: would we have the same success if we started teaching when the children were aged seven? The eight-year-olds had usually received one hour's specialist teaching per week, but we wondered if seven years was too young to start and whether, in any case, a whole hour was too long for children of that age. On the other hand, if we could get results somewhere near those that were achieved for the eight-year-olds, there was an obvious case for starting at age seven, since the children would, as it were, be a year ahead of the game.

It was possible to study in detail 10 seven-year-olds, eight boys and two girls, all of whom were severely retarded at reading and spelling and all of whom (bar one, for whom there was no record) showed characteristically dyslexic responses on the Bangor Dyslexia Test.

Eight out of the 10 made good progress – in the other two cases there seemed to be a combination of really adverse factors, and, since the progress of the eight was not significantly worse than that of the eight-year-olds who had already been taught by the unit's teachers (Chapter 5), we concluded that it would be advantageous in general if dyslexic children started their special teaching at age seven rather than at age eight.

In our report to the DES we recommended that there should be universal screening for literacy at age seven, that no child (other than the mentally handicapped) should leave class III without knowing the sounds of the individual letters, that when special tuition is given there should be full co-operation between the specialist teacher and the class teacher, that where possible the parents should be involved and encouraged to supplement the work of the specialist teacher and that the level of reading age on discharge should never be below nine as an absolute minimum.

We concluded the summary of our recommendations by saying: 'The procedures which we have described are economical in that they involve individual lessons only once per week and, since the teachers are peripatetic, no cost for the maintenance of buildings. The success rate, however, is high. In the light of the present data and those supplied by [Hornsby and Miles (1980)] we believe it to be around 80–85%. Steps are now needed to ensure that this relatively cheap form of help is provided on a nation wide scale.' Our full report will be found in Miles and Miles (1983b).

Elaine and I also had the opportunity to contribute a section on dyslexia to a book on developmental disorders among Kerala children (see Miles and Miles, 1999b).

AGE OF VOCABULARY ACQUISITION

There was a large amount of anecdotal evidence that dyslexics were late in learning to talk, but I owe to my colleague John Done an ingenious way of establishing the matter experimentally and quantifying the amount of lateness.

The argument is a somewhat complex one, and for full details readers should consult the original paper (Done and Miles, 1988). In brief, the starting point was an earlier finding that, in adults, there was a high correlation between the time which it took to name a picture (the 'response latency') and the age at which the name had been learned. We wondered if the same would be true in the case of dyslexic children. John started by giving 65 pictures to 101 children aged two, three, four and five years and noting in which age band (six-monthly intervals) 75% of the pictures could be named; the children were simply asked to say 'what the picture was called'. Some of the pictures were of objects likely to be known to the children but where the names were not all that high in tables of word frequencies, for example 'bicycle', 'giraffe' and 'windmill'. This was because John wanted to determine whether word frequency or age of acquisition was the more important factor. By a suitable statistical technique it was possible to study the influence of these two factors separately, and, although there was, of course, a correlation between the two, statistical analysis showed that age of acquisition was the more important.

After initially presenting these pictures to children John started on the main experiment. This involved giving the same 65 pictures to dyslexic and control subjects aged about 14.6. (The controls were marginally younger, so that, if there were any effect of age, it would count against the hypothesis which we were testing.) The response latencies of both groups correlated highly with the previously determined age of acquisition. However, the response latencies of the dyslexics were considerably longer than those of the controls. Overall, when he took into account the age of acquisition of the different words, John found that the difference in response latencies between the two groups produced an overall difference score of 67 milliseconds; this was found to represent a relative lateness in word acquisition score for the dyslexics of 10.8 months (note 15.6). This would seem to make sense as an overall measure of dyslexics' relative lateness in acquiring vocabulary.

DYSLEXICS' ORAL LANGUAGE

When I was giving the Picture Completion subtest of the Wechsler (1974) Intelligence Scale for Children – Revised, Eileen Stirling, who was sitting in with me as part of her M.Ed. course, noticed that when the children were asked to name the part which was missing from the picture many of them avoided the necessity for naming by pointing – correctly – to the missing part and saying, 'That bit.' It occurred to Eileen that this was something which might be worth studying in its own right: how good were dyslexics at word-finding? She checked on this, using 21 dyslexics and 19 controls (note 15.7). All the subjects were boys and were aged between 12 and 16 years.

In her first experiment she presented the subjects with cards containing pictures, and she asked her subjects to name the part of a card to which an arrow was pointing, e.g. the mane of a horse or the buckle of a shoe. (It was important that the words were not too familiar; otherwise boys of this age would have found them too easy.)

What Eileen found surprised her. In untimed conditions the dyslexics were no worse than the controls at producing something like the right word, but the reproduction of the word was sometimes inaccurate; for instance when the correct answer was 'buckle' (of a shoe), two dyslexic boys said 'buttle', while when the answer should have been 'hand' (of a watch) one boy said 'handle'. There were 11 such errors among the dyslexics and only one among the controls (note 15.8).

She then went on to try to find out how easy it was in the case of homonyms (e.g. bat/bat) or homophones (e.g. sale/sail) for the dyslexics to 'shift' from one meaning of a word to another. The task was to say what a particular word meant, and she told them that some of the words had two meanings and that, if they knew a second meaning, they were to give it.

Again the result surprised her. 'Shifting' was not a problem for the dyslexics, but there were many inaccurate pronunciations and some very curious grammatical expressions. Here are a few examples. In response to *place* ('plaice') one boy said, 'It can be a plaice of fish.' In reply to *peer* ('pier') one boy said, 'Appear in the door', while another said, 'A pier is what people walk along and fishing off.' One boy said that a *crocus* could be 'a plant or a game' – he was presumably thinking of *croquet* – and in response to *chip* one boy said it was something you gave to a waiter. There were virtually no similar curiosities among the controls.

It is not in dispute that dyslexics are fluent orally, but Eileen's study, where the responses were tape-recorded, shows that their oral language is far from flawless. Failure to distinguish between *hand* and *handle*, *crocus* and *croquet* and *chip* and *tip* suggests a lack of ability to differentiate between speech sounds, which is yet further evidence of their weakness in the area of phonology.

DYSLEXIC STUDENTS AT COLLEGE

Dr Kate Rook, who was a member of the secretarial staff, kept records of what happened to all the dyslexic students who took their degrees at the University of Wales, Bangor, during the years 1995–1998. They numbered 196, though this figure does not include 22 who left college before their final year or took time out. There were 188 who successfully obtained degrees; five sat the examination and failed, while three left college during their final year. This represents a 95.9% success rate. During this three-year period one dyslexic student obtained first-class honours while 74 obtained upper seconds.

DYSLEXIA IN THE KANNADA LANGUAGE

I was lucky to have the opportunity to collaborate with two colleagues, S. Ramaa (whose Ph.D. I had examined) and M. S. Lalithamma. Kannada is a Dravidian language spoken in some parts of India. We were particularly interested to discover if the manifestations of dyslexia were basically the same in a part of the world where there was a different writing system and where English was not the child's first language (note 15.9).

For full details of what we did the reader is referred to Ramaa *et al.* (1993). In brief, some 550 children in schools within a radius of 50 miles from Mysore were tested on 10 different tasks. As examples we may cite visual discrimination, auditory discrimination, recall of auditorily presented digits and sound blending. We specified a number of what we called 'basic exclusionary criteria', for example no children were included unless they were at least eight years old and had been attending school regularly. We ended up with 14 normal readers, 14 children believed to be dyslexic and 14 poor readers believed not to be dyslexic. The non-dyslexic poor readers were picked out partly because their reading retardation was less severe and, more importantly, because they were adjudged to have acquired certain basic skills in decoding and blending. To qualify as a dyslexic the child's retardation had to be more severe; they lacked these basic skills, and it was specified that they had to be receiving help at home, which meant that they were retarded despite this help.

Ten different tasks were set. Details will be found in the original paper, and I will limit myself to a discussion and description of four of them. They were:

1. An auditory discrimination test in which word pairs were presented auditorily, one member of the pair being confusable with the other, for instance *ippattu* (twenty) and *eppattu* (seventy). Each child was shown pictures of all the objects in advance and helped with naming them if this was necessary. Seventeen 'picture pairs' were used in various combinations. After the pair of sounds had been presented, the child was asked to point to the correct member of each 'picture pair'. The maximum possible score for this test was 17×4, that is 68.
2. A visual discrimination test, in which the child was presented with a card containing four, five or six items, only two of which were the same shape. The child was required to point to the two items having the same shape. Thirty cards were used, and one point was awarded for each correct response.
3. A recall-of digits test in which between two and eight digits were presented auditorily at the rate of two per second. The maximum possible score was 28.
4. A word analysis test in which single words are presented auditorily and the child is asked to analyse them into their component sounds. The maximum possible score was 33. The results are set out in Table 15.6.

On tests of visual and auditory discrimination there were no differences between the three groups. This is not surprising, given that the tasks did not involve naming or any kind of phonological skill. There were differences, however, between dyslexics and normal readers in their ability to recall auditorily presented digits and at breaking words into their components, and in the latter task the dyslexics also differed from the non-dyslexic poor readers. (For confidence levels see note 15.10.)

Table 15.6. Comparison of dyslexics, non-dyslexic poor readers and normal achievers on four different tasks, with standard deviations in brackets

Task	Dyslexics	Non-dyslexic poor readers	Normal readers
Visual discrimination	28.85 ± 7.18	20.07 ± 1.07	28.85 ± 1.17
Auditory discrimination	63.00 ± 3.64	63.93 ± 2.65	65.43 ± 4.64
Recall of digits	15.78 ± 1.48	18.07 ± 2.35	21.64 ± 5.27
Sound blending	21.35 ± 6.78	27.00 ± 4.15	29.64 ± 3.22

Adapted from Ramaa *et al.* (1993)

This study is one of the few, other than those reported in Chapter 20 of this book, where a distinction is drawn between dyslexics and those who are poor readers for other reasons, and it is interesting that on some of the tests the differences in score between these two groups were statistically significant. Our results also suggest that the manifestations of dyslexia are not basically different in Mysore from what they are in Britain. Our data are compatible with the thesis that dyslexia is a worldwide phenomenon which presents itself in much the same way in different parts of the world.

NOTES

Notes 15.1   I am particularly grateful to the following (in order of the research reported): Ann Williams, Beve Hornsby, Elaine Miles, Eileen Stirling, John Done and S. Ramaa.

Note 15.2   The confidence levels for the differences between dyslexics and controls in the Rorschach study were as follows: total number of responses U = 2, p < 0.002; for percentage of 'form' responses U = 19, p < 0.002; for number of card turnings U = 3, p < 0.002. All tests were two-tailed. When the total numbers of dyslexics and controls who did and did not turn the cards were compared, the dyslexics turned the cards less frequently (Fisher Exact Probability test p < 0.005).

Note 15.3   This description owes its origin to Margaret Rawson. Margaret was insistent, in particular, that the teaching should be multisensory, and this has been amply confirmed in practice. Hornsby and Miles (1980) quote one version of this description on pp. 236–237 of our paper.

Note 15.4   I am grateful to my former colleague, Dr Peter Harzem, for having shown me the usefulness of this kind of methodology. The same methodology, incidentally, has been used in the study of the behaviour of rats, for instance if the rat pressed a lever it might receive a food pellet. In the case of rats it is usually possible also to carry out a 'reversal' stage in which the intervention is withdrawn. If the rate of lever pressing then decreases, one can be very confident that the intervention caused the increase in lever pressing. Because of humans' ability to verbalise and recall, it is not always possible to obtain meaningful results if one uses the reversal phase in humans.

Note 15.5   If rate of reading gain before teaching is symbolised as RB and rate of reading gain during teaching as RD, for 102 children the mean difference was 1.40 (s.d. 1.10, t = 12.8, df 101, p < 0.001). For spelling, the corresponding figures for 107 children were: RB-RD 1.62 (s.d. 1.10, t = 15.0, df 106, p < 0.001).

Note 15.6   The calculation was done as follows. When the regression analysis was re-run with all the data combined, a regression coefficient of 37.3 was obtained, that is 37.3 units of latency for one unit of age of acquisition. Since each unit of age of acquisition represents six months, a difference of 67 m/sec represents 6 x 67/37.3 months, which comes to 10.8 months.

Note 15.7 The original intention was to compare 20 dyslexics with 20 controls. Eileen noticed, however, that a boy who had been given to her as a control gave her the impression of being dyslexic (her experience of dyslexics was considerable). On enquiry she found that the school had made a mistake and that there was, indeed, evidence that the boy was dyslexic. Since the matter was unlikely to make any difference to her statistics, we agreed that the boy should be classed as dyslexic.

Note 15.8 Chi-squared (1 df) = 6.83, p < 0.01.

Note 15.9 Those interested in the way in which dyslexia manifests itself in different languages may like to consult Miles and Miles (1999b, Chapter 5) and E. Miles (2000).

Note 15.10 Confidence levels were as follows: visual discrimination, all three groups, F = 0.18 (ns); auditory discrimination, all three groups, F = 1.84 (ns); recall of digits, F = 9.67 (p < 0.05); word analysis, F = 10.09 (p < 0.01). Post hoc t-tests showed that the dyslexics differed from the normal readers on recall of digits (t = 3.68, p < 0.01) and on word analysis (t = 3.67, p < 0.01). The dyslexics did not differ significantly from the non-dyslexic poor readers on recall of digits (t = 1.44, ns) but differed on word analysis (t = 2.50, p < 0.05).

16 The Dyslexic Adult

In the early 1970s a working party was set up to consider the needs of the dyslexic adult. The commissioning body was the British Council for the Rehabilitation of the Disabled. Its chairman was Dr Jan Kershaw. The Kershaw Committee reported in 1974.

At this time we had acquired some knowledge of the dyslexic child, but our knowledge of the dyslexic adult was extremely limited. However, by interpolating from our knowledge of the dyslexic child it was possible for us to make some comments and recommendations.

The report calls attention to the need for more adequate provision: 'We are greatly concerned that provision for the identification of dyslexic children is, at the present time, grossly inadequate' (p. 117). Other comments include: 'In general, the earlier appropriate remedial care and treatment are begun the greater is the prospect of success' (p. 117), a recommendation that there should be 'training of all the disciplines involved in the team aspects of the work' (p. 118), and a further recommendation that 'equally urgent attention be given to the better organisation of this work' (p. 118).

I myself have been able to investigate the needs of dyslexic adults by involving those reading for honours degrees in psychology at Bangor. There was available a panel of students, dyslexic and non-dyslexic, who had declared themselves available to assist with research. Many useful pilot studies were carried out by this means, and in a few cases it was possible for me to help the student to write the paper up for publication. Three such papers will be reported in what follows.

1. MATCHING SENTENCES WITH SYMBOLS

The first study, which will be found in Miles (1986), was one in which the data were collected and analysed by Joyce McCulloch. It involved presenting dyslexic adults and matched controls with a sentence and various marks or symbols. Sample stimuli are given in Figures 16.1 and 16.2.

There was a choice of two keys: if the sentence and the diagram were congruent, the subjects had to press one key (to signify 'true'); if the two were incongruent, they had to press the other key (to signify 'false'). It will be seen that in the case of Figure 16.1 the correct answer is 'true', while in the case of Figure 16.2 it is 'false'. All responses were timed, accurate measurement now being possible by means of a computer program.

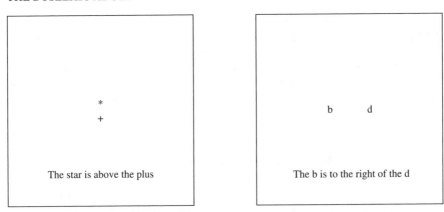

Figures 16.1 and 16.2.   Sample stimuli used in the matching experiment.

These tests were given to eight dyslexic college students and 14 suitably matched controls. The error rate was negligible. Of particular interest were the results of tests involving 'b' and 'd' and 'left' and 'right'. Sample data are set out in Table 16.1. The time is given in seconds and fractions of a second to three significant figures.

It will be seen that, whatever the stimuli, the dyslexics needed more time than the controls before they could respond correctly. The difference was more marked in the case of 'b' and 'd' and 'left' and 'right' than it was in the case of 'above' and 'below' or 'star' and 'plus'. Statistical analysis showed that the left–right and 'b'–'d' tasks were differentially more difficult for the dyslexics (note 16.1). As far as the other tasks were concerned, the dyslexics were always slower but there were no other tasks which they found **extra** difficult.

These results confirmed the view, widely accepted among those with experience of dyslexia, that the distinction between 'above' and 'below' causes fewer problems for dyslexics than the distinction between 'left' and 'right'. This is presumably because 'above' and 'below' remain the same whichever way one is facing, whereas 'left'

Table 16.1. Response times in seconds for dyslexics and controls to various combinations of stimuli

	Dyslexics	Controls
* +	3.882	2.129
b–d	5.984	2.473
Left	5.450	2.405
Right	5.245	2.377
Above	3.619	2.007
Below	3.624	2.125

Adapted from Miles (1986)

and 'right' do not. There is therefore the opportunity for regular and uninterrupted learning of 'above' and 'below' (and of 'up' and 'down'), whereas what is on the left from one point of view is on the right from another.

In the case of the 'star' and the 'plus' one must suppose that, at least for some subjects, only matching was necessary, not any naming. This would explain why the dyslexics' response times to 'star' and 'plus' are shorter than those to 'b' and 'd' and 'left' and 'right'.

2. COLOUR-NAMING EXPERIMENTS

From earlier research, for instance Denckla and Rudel (1976), there was reason to believe that if dyslexics were presented with a card containing familiar colours and asked to name them they would be slower at doing so than suitably matched controls. The reason for this, however, was not clear. One possibility was that in dyslexics the transmission of information through the nervous system is slower, with the result that, colour for colour, dyslexics take longer time. However, I had sometimes had the opportunity to observe dyslexics in a colour-naming task, and it seemed to me possible that, colour for colour, they might be no slower than controls but that they might become 'tied up' at certain stages of the task – perhaps through being overwhelmed by the effort called for in continually having to find the right name. In that case their longer overall time would be the result of extra long delays over a small number of colours, rather than a slight slowness over each individual colour. I therefore suggested to Samantha Gibbons that she might explore this possibility as a final-year student project. The eventual outcome was a paper published in *Dyslexia Review* (Miles and Gibbons, 2002).

We referred to the two possibilities mentioned above as the 'slow transmission' hypothesis and the 'glitch' hypothesis. By this time, fortunately, the technology was available which permitted the exact measurement of response times to individual colours (note 16.2). When sound was present, it produced the appropriate wave forms but not when the sound was absent. Wave forms would therefore appear as the subject named the colours but not in the pauses between the colour names. It was then possible to convert the distance between one 'trough' in the wave form and the next into a timescale; this showed the time needed for naming individual colours.

A card was prepared containing 40 coloured squares (five rows, eight columns), each 2 cm by 2 cm. Six different colours were used – red, black, orange, yellow, blue and green. To ensure that there was no uncertainty over the colour names these were told to the subjects in advance of the experiment. The subjects were asked to name all the colours on the card as quickly as they could.

In analysing the results it was necessary in the first place to specify how long the delay in naming a colour had to be before it counted as a glitch. We then had to check, first, whether the dyslexics needed more time than the controls to complete the task as a whole and, secondly, whether there were more glitches among the dyslexics than among the controls and, thirdly, if the times for the glitches were

Table 16.2. Times in seconds taken by dyslexics and controls in a colour-naming task

	Dyslexics	Controls
N	15	15
Mean	25.72	19.86
Standard deviation	5.21	4.35
Range	19–34	12–29

Adapted from Miles and Gibbons (2002)

Table 16.3. Total and median number of glitches on the part of dyslexics and controls at the three different criteria

Glitches of	Number	Dyslexics	Controls
0.4 sec. and over	Total	153	76
	Median	8	5
0.6 sec. and over	Total	76	25
	Median	4	2
0.8 sec. and over	Total	44	9
	Median	1	0

Adapted from Miles and Gibbons (2002)

removed from the calculation, whether the dyslexics would still be slower overall than the controls.

The definition of a glitch had to be made post hoc, that is when we already had the results available. To reduce the risk of misleading ourselves we differentiated between three types of glitches: those of 0.4 to 0.6 seconds, those between 0.6 and 0.8 seconds and those longer than 0.8 seconds.

A comparison between dyslexics and controls in respect of overall time is given in Table 16.2, a comparison in respect of the number of glitches in Table 16.3, and in Table 16.4 a comparison between the two groups when the glitch times were removed.

For technical statistical reasons it was necessary in Tables 16.3 and 16.4 to use a measure known as the 'median'. This measure is a form of average in which there is the same number of readings above a particular point in the distribution as below it.

Table 16.4. Median scores for dyslexics and controls with all glitches at 0.4 seconds and over removed

Dyslexics	Controls
0.20	0.14

Adapted from Miles and Gibbons (2002)

From these three tables it can be seen that the dyslexics were, indeed, slower than the controls in the total time taken to name the colours (note 16.3). This is in line with previous findings. By all three criteria for a glitch the dyslexics had a larger number of glitches (note 16.4). Finally, when all glitches of 0.4 seconds or more were taken out of the analysis the dyslexics still took longer than the controls to name the colours (note 16.5). It seems, therefore, that both hypothesised factors were at work: the longer overall times taken by the dyslexics can be attributed both to slower transmission time and to a larger number of glitches.

3. RECALL OF SENTENCES

In Miles (1993a, pp. 138–9) I note that when I gave my subjects sentences to remember from the Terman-Merrill (1960) test they were often able to report the gist of the sentence correctly but did not get the exact words right. When this happened, I said the sentence over again and asked them to have another try. What I found was that in some cases they needed as many as five or six repetitions before they were word perfect. This seemed a good idea for a student project, and I enlisted the help of two final-year students to check whether for the correct recall of sentences dyslexics needed more repetitions than controls (note 16.6).

Four sentences were chosen from the Terman–Merrill (1937) test. (Roman numerals in brackets indicate the mental age level based on the original test norms.)

Sentence 1 (year viii)
Billy has made a beautiful boat out of wood with his sharp knife.
Sentence 2 (year ix)
Yesterday we went for a ride in our car along the road that crosses the bridge.
Sentence 3 (Average Adult)
The red headed woodpeckers made a terrible fuss as they tried to drive the young away from the nest.
Sentence 4 (Superior Adult III)
At the end of the week the newspaper published a complete account of the experiences of the great explorer.

The subjects were 48 college students, 24 of them dyslexic. If a sentence was repeated correctly, the experimenter went on to the next sentence; if the response was incorrect, the experimenter read it again to the subject, if necessary several times, until the subject's response was 100% correct. A record was kept of the number of repetitions needed for correct recall.

We found that the dyslexics needed many more repetitions than the controls. The number of repetitions needed for each of the four sentences is set out in Table 16.5.

All differences were highly significant (note 16.7). We found that no control participant needed more than four repetitions for any one sentence or more than eight repetitions overall (that is in total over the four sentences). In contrast, only six dyslexics needed fewer than eight repetitions in total.

Table 16.5. Number of repetitions needed by dyslexic and control subjects for correct responding to each of the four sentences

Group	Sentence 1	Sentence 2	Sentence 3	Sentence 4	Total
Dyslexics	41	63	70	131	305
Controls	4	11	20	43	78

Adapted from Miles *et al.* (in press)

The performance of the dyslexics was very uneven. For instance, one subject could not repeat Sentence 2 correctly, even after 24 attempts, but needed no repetitions for Sentence 3 and only one for Sentence 4.

We suggested in our paper (Miles *et al.*, in press) that semantic satiation (which was mentioned in Chapter 3) may have been playing a part when very large numbers of repetitions were needed; this is the phenomenon whereby a word loses its meaning when it is repeated many times over. Overall, I think one has to conclude that dyslexics are more vulnerable than non-dyslexics: they may manage adequately on one occasion and not on another.

Hampshire (1981) suggests that dyslexics may have 'good days' and 'bad days'. The present results suggest that poor performance is not just something which happens on one day and not on another. It seems rather that within the same hour things can at one moment go reasonably right and at another moment go hopelessly wrong.

We also carried out an analysis of the different types of error made, for instance errors of omission, substitution, failure to complete the sentence etc. Overall the dyslexics made a total of 902 errors in the different types combined, compared with 125 by the controls. Allowing for the greater number of errors made by the dyslexics overall, we still found that omission errors (that is leaving out words) were proportionally more frequent among the dyslexics. In contrast, the proportion of substitution errors (that is substituting a different word in place of the correct one) was no different from that of the controls.

The conclusion appears to be that dyslexics are poor at attending to detail but are unimpaired at processing for meaning.

RECOLLECTIONS

A. It was a privilege to be invited to serve on this committee, and I had the chance to meet regularly with my mentor, Professor Oliver Zangwill, and with Dr Alfred White Franklin, whom I now knew well as a consequence of our meetings in connection with the Word-Blind Centre. In addition to the chairman of the working party, Dr Kershaw, and the vice-chairman, Ian Henderson, the members of the working party included Guy Gray, a psychologist working in the Department of Employment, Colin Stevenson, who had been an education officer in the army,

Sandhya Naidoo (author of Naidoo, 1972), Gill Cotterell, whom I knew from our Word-Blind Centre days, and, not least, the dedicated secretary to the working party, Dorothy Pammenter. Guy, Colin, Gill and Sandhya are still alive today and have remained lifelong friends. One of the people who gave evidence to the committee was the actress Susan Hampshire, who afterwards visited me in Bangor and has referred to my work in Hampshire (1981).

B.   On one occasion I gave the 'b'–'d' 'star'–'plus' test to a dyslexic university lecturer. His initial responses were slow enough to be regarded as typically dyslexic. Suddenly, however, about halfway through the testing, they speeded up. He afterwards explained to me that he had suddenly thought of a more efficient strategy: it was unnecessary to name both the 'b' (or 'd') and the 'left' (or 'right'). If the two 'pictures' on the left matched (they did not have to be named) and the word 'right' appeared, he was to press the 'false' button, whereas if the word 'left' appeared, he was to press the 'true' button. This seemed to me to be a striking demonstration that dyslexics take longer when stimuli have to be named. I also realised that nature sometimes plays tricks on those who wish to experiment using repeated measures. If there is a change of strategy part way through, the resultant statistics are not easily usable.

I presented the 'b–d' and 'star–plus' material at a talk and was dismayed to learn that the speaker who was due to follow me reported that he himself found the test extremely hard. I was dismayed, thinking that perhaps, after all, it was not as good a test for picking out dyslexics as I had supposed. I was much relieved, however, when in the ensuing talk he started to write on the blackboard – he explained that he was dyslexic!

NOTES

Note 16.1   Detailed statistical analysis of the results will be found in Miles (1986). Analysis of variance showed that the dyslexics took longer overall than the controls ($p < 0.001$), and, in addition, there were significant interactions between group (dyslexic vs. control) $\times$ condition (left–right) ($p < 0.001$) and 'b'–'d' ($p < 0.001$). All other interactions were non-significant.

Note 16.2   We used an Apple Macintosh computer with a Mac recorder which recorded the subjects' oral responses as wave forms. Samantha and I are grateful to Professor Rod Nicolson for supplying us with this device.

Note 16.3 $t = 3.35$, $p < 0.01$.

Note 16.4   Criterion > 0.4 seconds: $U = 58.5$, $p < 0.05$; criterion > 0.6 seconds: $U = 54.5$, $p < 0.01$; criterion > 0.8 seconds: $U = 52.5$, $p < 0.01$.

Note 16.5 $U = 54.5$, $p < 0.01$.

Note 16.6   The project was undertaken by Judith (Jude) Roberts and Josie Schiffeldrin. Some years later, when the project was being written up with a view to publication, I was joined by my colleague Dr Guillaume

Thierry, whose contribution to the paper totally transformed it. I owe a large debt to all three.

Note 16.7   Confidence levels for the differences between dyslexics and controls over the four sentences were: Sentence 1: U = 136.5, p < 0.001; Sentence 2: U = 127, p < 0.001; Sentence 3: U = 167, p < 0.01; Sentence 4: U = 134, p < 0.001).

17 Talking Things Over

When parents brought their children to me for assessment, my usual procedure was to start by seeing both the parents and the child together for about 15 minutes. My first task was to try to put the child at their ease in front of their parents, since the experience of meeting a stranger in these circumstances was likely to be rather alarming. (To avoid unnecessary circumlocutions I shall assume in this chapter that the child is male.)

I quite often started by addressing my remarks to the child, for instance I might say: 'Is it your spelling that you have problems with?' Then, if he nodded, I would say something like, 'Don't worry, as I am used to seeing people with spelling problems. What I will try to do is to find out what things you are good at and what things you are less good at. Then we can see how best to help you with the things you are less good at.' During this initial interview it was also possible to give the parents the chance to indicate if there were any special points which they wanted me to investigate.

The child was then seen on his own for perhaps one to one and a half hours, after which he rejoined his parents. For about 15 minutes I scored up the results and examined the child's school exercise books, which I always asked the parents to bring. Then for an hour or longer I saw the parents and child together. I have come to realise over the years that the final hour was the most important part of the assessment.

I was quite willing to modify this procedure if there were special reasons for doing so. For example, if the child was young or seemed extra anxious, I sometimes invited the mother to be present during the whole of the assessment. However, this happened only rarely. During the time when I saw the parents and child together it was possible for the child to switch off and not listen if he was tired, but he sometimes sat up and took notice if I said something which seemed to him to be important.

I usually began by reporting to the parents the results of the reading and spelling tests. There were times during my later assessments when I wondered if I should use more up-to-date tests of reading and spelling than the Schonell tests, since these dated from 1952. However, I decided that the Schonell tests gave me what I needed, and, had I changed to different tests, this would have cast doubt on any comparisons which I might have made between my earlier results and my later ones.

I never pretended to a child that he had done well on a reading or spelling test if this was not the case. Given that the child was dyslexic, however, as was almost invariably the case (see note 17.1), I might sometimes say, for instance, 'Considering your handicap I think you have not done at all badly.' However, it would have been wrong to give the child or the parents erroneous information simply in order to be encouraging.

I also told them the results of the intelligence test. Here it was almost always possible to be positive. This was because, even if the child was of fairly limited ability as judged by the results of the intelligence test, some parents feared, not surprisingly, that their child's lack of literacy skills meant that he was simply slow. For this reason it was a relief for them to be told that this was not the case. It was also possible to call attention to their successes, for example relatively high subtest scores on the Wechsler or passes at a high level on the Terman–Merrill. This was clearly more informative than citing a 'global IQ', which, for reasons given in Chapter 9, I always considered a virtually meaningless measure in the case of dyslexic children. There were other children whom the parents knew to be bright; here they were often relieved to have this confirmed, particularly if they had been told otherwise by one of their child's teachers.

It was always interesting to go through the results of the Bangor Dyslexia Test. I sometimes asked if they had noticed anything similar to what I had picked up, for instance confusion over 'left' and 'right' or becoming 'tied up' when trying to repeat long words. If they had, it was then possible to tell them that this was part of the overall dyslexic picture.

Parents have sometimes said to me in irritation: 'Yes, he was assessed by an educational psychologist who told us he was intelligent but a poor reader and speller. This was of no help because we knew that already.' As a result of such comments I began to ask myself, 'What else does a diagnosis of dyslexia provide?'

One way, I think, of describing what I was giving to those whom I assessed and their families is what in Miles (1988) I call a 'hermeneutic' account of the position. *Hermeneus* is the Greek for 'interpreter', and I think that what I was doing was to interpret (or make sense of) occurrences of which they were already aware but whose significance they may not have fully appreciated.

I remember assessing a student who had previously been in the navy. When I gave him the 'left'–'right' items on the Bangor Dyslexia Test, he was immediately able to recall that his commanding officer had sworn at him for confusing 'port' and 'starboard'. What had been an isolated event suddenly made sense to him.

When this sort of thing happens, it is likely that other seemingly unrelated incidents will then be recognised as forming part of the same pattern – forgotten messages, for instance, mistakes over times and dates and the existence of similar difficulties in other members of the family. If what I said made sense to my subjects, I sometimes found that they were starting to make sense for themselves of other episodes in their lives.

During my training at the Tavistock Clinic I had been expressly warned about the dangers of giving advice. Advice, I was told, often falls on deaf ears because for personal reasons the person is unable to accept it. However, in my assessments for dyslexia it would have been inappropriate for me to be non-directive: I was being consulted on the grounds that I had specialist knowledge of dyslexia. I therefore did not hesitate to give advice, but what I regularly did was to ask if what I was saying made sense to my subjects. Almost invariably the answer was yes.

One of the situations where I found it necessary to tread carefully was that in which parents asked me to tell the head teacher of their child's school that their child was dyslexic – and then tell him or her what to do about it! When this arose, I asked the parents if they could so manage things that the head teacher wrote to me in the first place. I explained that it was inappropriate and might even be counterproductive if, uninvited, I appeared to be teaching my colleagues how to do their job. For the most part I found head teachers very cooperative.

In the case of a small number of dyslexic children (surprisingly few, in my judgement, in view of the pressures which they experience) there were significant behavioural problems. I was fairly confident, however, that, once the nature of the child's dyslexia was understood, family tensions would gradually lessen and the undesirable behaviour gradually disappear.

In talking to parents at the end of my assessments I continually had occasion to emphasise that once the overall picture was clear a great deal depended on common sense. Thus the fact that a child was carrying a constitutionally caused handicap did not mean that no standards at all were possible; rather, what was needed was an adjustment of standards on the part of both parents and teachers. As a result it was necessary to take account in particular of the fact that reading and writing were likely to be extra laborious and that the child was likely to tire easily. It was a matter of common sense not to press the child too far if he or she was tired.

Another common-sense point is that careful thought is needed as to how fast the child should be 'paced': if the school work is not up to his intellectual level, he will become bored, whereas if too much is expected too soon, he may not be able to cope. Experience suggests that it is better that dyslexics should be over-stretched, particularly if they are warned in advance of possible disappointments, rather than that they should not be stretched sufficiently. I recently heard a successful adult dyslexic say that many of the problems in his earlier life had arisen not from what he was unable to do but from what he had not been allowed to do. The best answer that I know to the question concerning the rate at which a child should be paced lies in the wise words of Margaret Rawson: 'Go as fast as you can and as slow as you must.'

It is also a matter of common sense to appreciate that children who are carrying a handicap may need extra comfort and reassurance from their parents at times of difficulty, and I frequently used to encourage mothers to back their own judgement when it came to the extra cuddle or extra attention rather than be influenced by well-meaning friends or even professional 'experts' who might say the child was too old for such things.

There is the further point that by emphasising the need for common sense one is thereby conveying to the parents that one trusts their judgement and that one is not there to find fault. I suspect that the popular image of psychologists and psychiatrists who unearth 'complexes' and criticise people for the terrible way in which they bring up their children is not wholly dead, and it is therefore useful to make clear by word and gesture that one is taking what the parents say at its face value.

I was sometimes asked about the value of tinted overlays. There is now good evidence that for some people, including some dyslexics, they make reading easier

(Miles and Miles, 1999a, Chapter 7), probably because they reduce the amount of glare coming up from the page. It was necessary, however, to warn against exaggerated claims, for instance that at long last a cure for dyslexia had been discovered.

Occasionally, too, I was asked whether I would advise the family to spend money on a 'new' kind of treatment for dyslexia – sometimes one which had recently achieved headlines in the popular press. I knew well that desperate parents are sometimes willing to spend just about their last penny in getting help for their dyslexic child. I wondered, therefore, if I had a duty to warn them against wasting their money.

In practice, if I had reservations about it, I was very hesitant to condemn a particular kind of treatment out of hand. It would have been unfair to those offering the treatment, and, for all I knew, I might have deprived the person being treated of some help. There was also the possibility of what doctors call the 'placebo effect', where a patient's belief that a treatment is effective may make it so, regardless of what is done or of what drug is prescribed. Rather than advise against such treatment, I would tend to say something like, 'Do not be too disappointed if it does not work.'

I have sometimes found it helpful to discuss with families the role of laughter. I have noticed over the years that those families for whom the dyslexia was causing least stress were often those who, in the most sympathetic way, were able to laugh at some of the things which went wrong. A father who is himself dyslexic and who says, 'My spelling is still darned awful' is first and foremost showing sympathy; and if, in addition, mother then says, 'Yes, you made a right mess of that letter to Aunt Jane, didn't you, dear?', this establishes that dyslexic-type errors will be understood rather than punished. As long as one is not laughing unsympathetically **at** the child but rather **with** him, one can help him to laugh at the things which sometimes go wrong. For instance, if you say with a laugh, 'You silly idiot! You've gone and muddled up left and right again!', this is basically a sympathetic comment since it shows understanding. It is my experience that in many different contexts laughter is often a very effective way of removing tension.

It was my usual practice when I carried out assessments not only to talk about immediate present needs but to try to forestall possible problems in the future. With this in mind I would sometimes say in the presence of the parents, even to quite young children, 'There may be people who tell you that you are lazy or stupid, but we know that you are **not** lazy or stupid.' To those contemplating college or university courses I might say something like: 'Don't be put off going to college by your well-meaning friends if you feel in your heart of hearts that that is what you want to do. When you have got there, you may feel moments of doubt as to whether you have done the right thing, and do not be surprised if this happens – it does not mean your choice was wrong.'

I end this chapter by offering a checklist. This is reproduced from Miles (1993b, pp. 91–92), at a time when I was trying to take stock of what I was doing during assessments. I pass this list on in the hope that others doing assessments for dyslexia will find it useful.

1. Was it made clear to the child at the start that he is not on trial, but that what is being done is aimed at helping?
2. Did you make clear that you sympathised with the parents in their struggles to get help?
3. Was any attempt made to remove the impression which they could have been given in the past that they were 'over-fussy'?
4. Was anything said about the extra comforting and reassurance needed by many dyslexic children?
5. Was anything said about social problems such as missed appointments and forgotten messages?
6. How much was said about the person's strong points? Was the issue of the person's intelligence discussed? Was the question considered as to whether the person's intelligence may have been underestimated both by themselves and by others?
7. Were the parents/child/adult asked if the diagnosis made sense to them?
8. Was any attempt made to forewarn against possible future problems and prepare the person for them?

RECOLLECTIONS

I remember being rather dismayed when I visited the USA in 1974 at the amount of time my American colleagues gave to assessing an individual child – at least a whole morning and sometimes a full day. At an early stage in my own research, however, I think I must have acquired a feel for what information was strictly relevant for my own limited purpose, which was to discover if the child was dyslexic and advise accordingly. I take the view that this can be determined relatively quickly once one knows what to look for. I will even confess to having sometimes made diagnoses over the telephone on the basis of a relatively small number of manifestations which the caller described to me. On one occasion the caller rang an experienced colleague of mine who reached the same conclusion. When parents wrote asking for an assessment for their child, I always made clear in reply that this was not a medical examination but only an examination for dyslexia.

With regard to safeguarding the future I had originally (Miles, 1988, 1993b) referred to these advance warnings as 'prophylactic' warnings, meaning warnings that might guard the person in advance. When I used this expression in a talk which I gave in the USA, however, my American colleague informed me that 'prophylactic' is understood in America to mean a condom. From then on I spoke simply of an 'advance' warning.

NOTE

Note 17.1   During the time when I was collecting the data for Miles (1993a) I tried to make sure that every individual whom I assessed was accounted for. Between 1972 and 1978 I had collected files on 291 children, of whom

I had adjudged 258 to be typically dyslexic and a further seven to be marginally so. Of the remaining seven, I judged three not to be dyslexic, the remaining 24 being either of limited ability or having problems other than typically dyslexic ones. Of these 24, 12 were male and 12 female, whereas of the 223 children for whom I had full records and whom I judged to be dyslexic the number of males was 182 and the number of females 41, a ratio of 4.4:1 (see Miles, 1993a, Chapter 4 for more details and Miles *et al.*, 1998, for more on gender ratio).

18 Proposal for a Taxonomy of Dyslexia

The word 'taxonomy' means 'way of classifying' or 'classificatory principle'. Although the word has been used primarily in biology and medicine, there is no reason why it should not be used more widely. How to classify anomalies of development is very much a live issue at the present time.

Classifications can be made for many different purposes. For a start, it seems to me helpful to draw a distinction between **strong** and **weak** taxonomies. I illustrate this distinction by a series of examples.

Let us suppose, in the first place, that the organiser of a conference needs to distinguish those who intend to go on an excursion and those who do not. There is, of course, nothing wrong with such a classification. On the other hand no one would be tempted to say it was a powerful or strong one; rather it is a classification made for a strictly limited purpose without any implication that it is of any lasting value. In particular there is no suggestion that biological markers – neurological or biochemical differences, for instance – will be discovered which differentiate excursion-goers from non-excursion-goers; nor would one expect biologists to classify them as 'two distinct species' or claim that the distinction heralded a significant scientific breakthrough. In practice the word 'taxonomy' is not used of cases of this kind, but, if it were, one would have to speak of an extremely weak taxonomy.

It would also be a manifestation of a weak taxonomy if someone were to classify a whale as a fish on the grounds that it lived in the sea, or a duck-billed platypus as a bird because it possessed a beak. In both cases it is known that there are a large number of anatomical features which point, beyond doubt, to the classification 'mammal'.

Medicine constitutes an interesting example because some of its taxonomies are very much stronger than others. For example, the terms 'fever' and 'nervous breakdown' still survive in common use since neither is wholly uninformative; if, however, they are contrasted with terms such as 'tuberculosis' and 'phenylketonuria' the differences are plain. It is characteristic of strong medical taxonomies that they imply a theory of causation, accurate prognosis and distinctive methods of treatment (compare the arguments in Davis and Cashdan, 1963, which were discussed in Chapter 11). Some taxonomies, one might say, are 'nosologic' and some 'nosographic' in the sense given to these words in Chapter 10. A strong or nosologic taxonomy is more than a description; it implies a full understanding of what is happening.

The word 'syndrome' is interesting in this connection. *Butterworth's Medical Dictionary* (Critchley, 1978, p. 1647) defines a syndrome as 'a distinct group of symptoms or signs which, associated together, form a characteristic clinical picture or entity'. Similarly *Churchill's Medical Dictionary* (Konigsberg, 1989, p. 1838) refers to 'signs, symptoms, or other manifestations' and adds that the word is 'used especially when the cause of the condition is unknown'. One can therefore say that use of the term 'syndrome' implies partial knowledge; it indicates that we are in possession of a taxonomy of moderate strength even though much more remains to be discovered.

If one makes classifications of any kind, this involves being both a 'lumper' and a 'splitter'. A lumper is one who wishes to group (or 'lump') certain phenomena together, whereas a 'splitter' is one who treats the phenomena under investigation as separate (or 'splits' them). The issue of substance in disputes over developmental anomalies of all kinds is where to 'lump' and where to 'split'.

There is no special merit either in lumping or in splitting as such. Hypothesis building may require us to lump together phenomena which seemed prima facie unconnected, and this can sometimes constitute a significant advance; on the other hand, as knowledge increases and researchers become more sensitive to differences, there may be increased pressures towards splitting. Whether one should be a lumper or a splitter will therefore depend on the circumstances of a particular case.

Once this point is recognised, the way becomes open for some of the apparent conflicts in disputed areas to be resolved: both parties may be right, since lumping may be appropriate for one purpose and splitting for another. Moreover, since boundaries often need to be changed as science advances, there is no need to fan the flames of controversy by insisting that a particular boundary is the only correct one to draw. This, however, does not justify a laissez-faire attitude towards the selection of a taxonomy. As has already been pointed out, some taxonomies are stronger than others, and, if one's objective is scientific research, it is inefficient to use a weaker taxonomy when a stronger one is available.

An analogy supplied by my colleague Professor Rod Nicolson may be of help in this connection. There are all kinds of places where one might apply pressure to a rock, but, if one applies pressure exactly along a fault line, any resultant division of the rock will provide meaningful 'chunks' for further study. In contrast, if one applies pressure in other places, one will be confronted merely with a collection of disconnected fragments, and it will be difficult to make sense of them.

There is a further reason why some taxonomies can be better than others. If a taxonomy is proposed from a position of strength – from a position of knowledge – a particular decision to lump or split merits nothing but respect. If two researchers are both aware of all the reasons for lumping and of all the reasons for splitting, even if one person decides to be a lumper and the other a splitter, there is nothing significant left for them to disagree about – at most there might be a disagreement about what similarities and differences are the important ones to emphasise. In contrast, if proposals for classification show a lack of such awareness, they can justifiably be faulted. I suspect that those who opposed the concept of dyslexia in the 1970s (see Chapters 11 and 12) were unaware of some of the reasons for lumping.

My thesis is that dyslexia is a syndrome – one which can supply a taxonomy of considerable strength if research findings in a number of areas are seen as interrelated and are therefore lumped together. The syndrome comprises a pattern of difficulties which is easily recognised once one knows what to look for. Its power lies in the fact that it encourages researchers to lump together a number of seemingly disparate phenomena. In particular there is anatomical evidence that dyslexics show some distinctive differences in brain organisation beyond the limits of normal variation; there is genetic evidence based on the fact that the same pattern of difficulties often runs in families, and there is the evidence for phonological difficulties, that is difficulties in the ordering, identification and remembering of speech sounds. The concept of dyslexia, in the sense given to it in this book, straddles these three research areas – anatomical research, genetic research and the behavioural research which points to the existence of a phonological deficit. Any advance in one of these areas is likely to be of help to the other two.

There remains the question of whether within the group of dyslexics there is any justification for further splitting. In Chapter 14 I reported that I could find no evidence for saying that 'visual dyslexics' were a different group from 'auditory dyslexics', and it is suggested in Miles and Miles (1994) that subtyping based on acquired dyslexia (deep dyslexics, surface dyslexics, phonological dyslexics) did not make much sense when applied to developmental dyslexia. Future research may, of course, suggest some different subtypes, but my personal view is that this is unlikely.

The demarcation of a taxonomy can be achieved either by coining a new word or by making stipulations about the more precise use of a current one. As the word 'dyslexia' lies ready to hand I propose to use it. There is now, I believe, enough consensus that dyslexia should be regarded as a syndrome, and not simply as a synonym for 'poor reading', to justify the stipulation to use the word in this way. A specially coined atheoretical term, such as 'the alpha syndrome', would have done as well, except for the fact that any theoretical link with the word 'dyslexia' would have been lost.

At present the links between these different research areas are suggestive rather than firmly proven. We do not know, for instance, whether the typical dyslexic who has been diagnosed on the basis of the Bangor Dyslexia Test (Miles, 1997) would usually or always be found to show distinctive patterns of activation if their brains were scanned. It is the sign of a strong taxonomy that it generates problems of this kind for research.

In contrast to all this my contention is that 'poor reading' provides only a very weak taxonomy; it lumps together a whole variety of phenomena which may have arisen from quite different causes and which may lead to quite different outcomes. As far as the concept of 'poor reading' is concerned there is no reason to be anything other than a splitter. This does not, of course, mean that the concept of 'poor reading' is never of any value to anyone. It may be that a Local Education Authority wishes to know the reading standards in the area for which it is responsible. Such enquiries may, of course, be of value, but they are not, and do not claim to be, the stuff of which scientific advances are made.

There is, however, a difficulty with my proposal for lumping which needs to be addressed. It is that much of the research into dyslexia has used 'poor reading' as a criterion for subject selection. It therefore seems inconsistent that in this book I have sometimes drawn on research findings based on poor reading as the criterion for dyslexia and then asserted that that criterion is unacceptable.

What I suspect has happened is that the great majority of the subjects investigated in these researches have been genuinely dyslexic. Those who are poor readers from lack of opportunity are a decreasing number, since, at least in Britain, the opportunities for learning to read are extremely widespread. The amount of 'noise' in the selection of subjects has, I suspect, been minimal. My quarrel is at the theoretical level: some researchers may not have used the word 'dyslexic' at all, and some of those who used it may have supposed that they were studying poor readers when in fact most of their subjects were manifesting the syndrome of dyslexia.

As we saw in Chapter 15, Ramaa *et al.* (1993) were able to draw a distinction between those poor readers who were and were not dyslexic, and one must suppose that lack of opportunity is more common in parts of India than it is in Britain. Attempts by myself and my colleagues to distinguish those with literacy problems who were and were not dyslexic will be reported in Chapters 19 and 20.

19 The British Births Cohort Study I

It was an exciting new venture when I was asked to take part in the 1980 follow-up of the 1970 British Births Cohort Study. This study related to all those children born in England, Wales and Scotland during the week 5–11 April 1970. There was a follow-up study in 1975, when the children were aged five, and a further follow-up in 1980, when they were aged 10.

The original number of children studied was 14 906. In 1980 the number was 12 905. The main reasons for this drop in numbers appear to have been the difficulty in tracing some families, their removal overseas and, sadly, in some cases, death.

At birth and in subsequent follow-up studies medical, social and, in 1980, educational data were obtained. My own involvement was in the follow-up in 1980; I was invited to explore what could be found out from the cohort study about the existence and nature of dyslexia (note 19.1).

The organisers of the study had already agreed that certain educational tests should be given to children when they reached age 10. They included a test of single word reading, a test of reading comprehension, which afterwards became the Edinburgh Reading Test (1985), a spelling test in the form of a dictation and tests of non-word reading and non-word spelling. Non-words – sometimes called 'nonsense words' or 'pseudowords' – are combinations of letters which do not spell actual words but which are pronounceable. They are included in many research studies on the grounds that they test the person's knowledge of letter–sound correspondences and their ability to use analogies with familiar words. In the present study examples of the eight non-words to be read included 'ronumental' and 'teague'. The four non-words which had to be spelled were 'prunty', 'slimber', 'grondel' and 'blomp'.

There was also a mathematics test, a test of whether the child could understand the significance of pictures and four items from the British Ability Scales (BAS) (Elliott *et al.*, 1983) (note 19.2). These were: Similarities, Matrices, Recall of Digits and Word Definitions.

The scores on these tests were standardised so as to give a mean (average) of 100 and a standard deviation of 15. This made it possible to know whether a particular child was above or below average on a given test and to ensure comparability between tests.

I took the view that a necessary condition for a diagnosis of dyslexia was poor reading or spelling in relation to intelligence. In choosing a measure of intelligence it was necessary to bear in mind the existence of the so-called ACID profile (see Chapter 9) and the general danger that on some of the traditional tests of intelligence dyslexic children might obtain scores that did not do justice to their intellectual level.

Fortunately I had had the opportunity to see in advance some work by my colleague Dr Michael Thomson on the performance of dyslexics on the BAS (note 19.3). Michael found that on some items the dyslexics in his group scored above the average as determined by the published norms and on some items below it. He found that on both the Similarities and Matrices tests his subjects scored above average. Since in the British Births Cohort study scores were available on both these tests, we decided that they should be used in conjunction as a measure of intelligence. We therefore standardised the combined scores on the Similarities and Matrices tests so that, like the other tests (see above), it should have a mean (average) of 100 and a standard deviation of 15.

With some hesitation, we decided to exclude from our main analyses of the data those children with scores on the Similarities and Matrices tests of less than 90. This was not because we believed that children of low intelligence could not be dyslexic but because we thought that in their case there might be complicating factors which were not typical of dyslexics within the average ability range.

The test of single-word reading (word recognition) seemed preferable to the Edinburgh Reading test; the latter involved comprehension and there was reason to believe that dyslexics were unimpaired at this. Such a test would not therefore reveal the full extent of their reading disability. We also decided to pay particular attention to the spelling scores, on the grounds that a child who was spelling adequately at age 10 could not be severely dyslexic. To qualify as a dyslexic, therefore, a child had either to be a severe underachiever at spelling regardless of their score on the word recognition test or a moderate underachiever at spelling who was also a severe underachiever at word recognition.

On the basis of scores on the Similarities and Matrices tests on the one hand and scores on the word recognition test and spelling tests on the other we divided the cohort into three groups – normal achievers, moderate underachievers and severe underachievers (note 19.4).

As possible indicators of dyslexia it was agreed to include items from the Bangor Dyslexia Test, the first edition of which was due to be published in 1982. A decision had therefore to be made as to which of the 10 items to choose. The constraints were that there was time for only about three items and that their administration should be straightforward, since they were to be given to the children by their class teachers. We had therefore to choose items which could most easily be administered in a standardised way.

The items which we eventually chose were Left–Right, Months Forwards and Months Reversed. The Recall of Digits item from the BAS had already been included (see above), and it made sense that we should add this test to the other three, since there was already good evidence that poor readers also performed poorly on this item (Miles and Ellis, 1981, p. 230). In earlier times it had been assumed that ability to recall digits was an indication of intelligence, but by now it was plain that many highly intelligent dyslexics often found this task difficult.

We decided to refer to these four items as the 'supplementary' items, since they provided a supplement to the rest of the educational data. We did not at this stage wish to beg any questions by calling them the 'dyslexia' items, since we believed that they could be regarded as indicators of dyslexia only in the context of severe underachievement. In a current paper, for ease of reference, we have used the expression 'possible indicators (of dyslexia)', abbreviated to PIs (Haslum and Miles, in press). Specified responses were indicators of dyslexia only in the appropriate context.

It is not at all easy, of course, in a survey on this scale to avoid mishaps, and we do not know how much our results were contaminated by 'noise' resulting from teachers' failures to follow the instructions to the letter (note 19.5). However, the size of the population studied made it unlikely that such mishaps, if they occurred, would seriously affect our results.

Our first task was to specify how children whom we believed to be dyslexic should be picked out. If we simply showed that some children had reading and/or spelling problems, or even unexpected reading or spelling problems in view of their intelligence, this would have provided no justification for claiming that they were dyslexic in the required sense. To adopt the terminology used in Chapter 10, if it were to be of any use, the word 'dyslexia' needed to contain 'bite' and, in the terminology of Chapter 18, provide a strong taxonomy. If the dyslexia concept were to achieve this, it would lead to findings which we could not otherwise have predicted or discovered. We had therefore to decide what definition of dyslexia would generate interesting questions and make possible their investigation, given the basic components of the syndrome as described in Chapter 18.

It was also important that we should not make a stipulation which departed widely from the commonly accepted meaning of the word 'dyslexia', in so far as there was one. In this connection we needed to follow the advice of the philosopher Sidgwick (1922, p. 264) quoted in Chapter 7. Sidgwick made the general point that it was in order to make our ordinary concepts more precise as long as we did not depart too far from ordinary usage – 'We may, so to speak, clip the ragged edge of common usage, but we must not make excision of any considerable portion.'

In the present context what was needed was to operationalise the concept of dyslexia, that is provide a set of operations in terms of which its presence or absence could be determined – in such a way that we were not departing too far from the commonly accepted meaning of the word. As will be seen from Chapter 20 we in fact ended up by making proposals that the boundaries of the concept of dyslexia needed to be revised, but at least our starting point had to be the commonly accepted meaning of the word. It would then be necessary to test hypotheses as to ways in which dyslexics and non-dyslexics might be different. In this way, were scientifically important differences to be found, progress would most certainly be being made.

It was also important, in this connection, to conform to Popper's principle of falsifiability (Popper, 1963, p. 36): it was logically incumbent on us to specify what outcomes would indicate that we were **wrong**. Then, if these outcomes failed to occur, we could say that our attempts to knock down a particular hypothesis had been to that extent unsuccessful. Those who claimed that the hypothesis was wrong were left with facts which somehow or other they would need to explain away.

On the basis of my clinical experience I had reached the conclusion that typical dyslexics were those who were retarded at reading and spelling in relation to their intelligence and who additionally showed positive indicators on the Bangor Dyslexia Test. There would not be the same opportunity for detailed examination in the British Births Cohort Study, since there were only four 'dyslexia' items in place of the 10 which were available in the Bangor Dyslexia Test, and there would not be any opportunities for me to observe the children at first hand or give further tests. However, I had reasonable confidence on clinical grounds that the four supplementary items were relevant to dyslexia in the sense of the word which I needed. It was therefore a question of finding out if dyslexia-positive responses to these items were related to other findings.

Although at the time I thought of dyslexia as an 'all or none' phenomenon – either you were dyslexic or you were not – I decided that it was necessary to have what we called a 'buffer' group – those who were possibly dyslexic but about whom there was some doubt. In addition to subdividing the children into normal achievers, moderate underachievers and severe underachievers, therefore, my colleagues and I also subdivided the children into three groups based on their performance on the supplementary items. For this purpose we used the method of scoring which had been devised for the Bangor Dyslexia Test, where a typically dyslexic response was scored as 'plus', a marginally dyslexic response as 'zero' and a response free from any indicators of dyslexia as 'minus'. On the Bangor Dyslexia Test a 'zero' was scored as half a 'plus', so that a diagnosis of dyslexia could be made either on a relatively small number of major indicators or a rather larger number of minor ones.

For purposes of the British Births Cohort Study we decided that those with two or more 'pluses' or three or more 'zeros' on the supplementary items, if they were also severe underachievers, should constitute our dyslexic group; those with two 'zeros' or a 'plus' and a 'zero' should belong to the buffer group, while the remainder, comprising those with a single 'plus', a single 'zero' or no positive indicators at all, should be put into a third group. For ease of reference we designated those with two or more pluses or three or more 'zeros' as 'underachievers A', those in the buffer group as 'underachievers B' and the remainder as 'underachievers C'. We later extended this A, B and C classification to the moderate underachievers and the normal achievers, since we found some interesting results among those who came out as normal achievers but who, nevertheless, were showing positive indicators on the supplementary items.

A dyslexic was therefore defined as a severe underachiever at word recognition or spelling who had two or more 'pluses' or three or more 'zeros' on the supplementary items. We did not wish to claim that the boundaries marked by the A, B and C categories were firm ones; it was rather that, if the supplementary items were of value, among the severe underachievers there would be a greater proportion of typical dyslexics in the A group and fewest in the C group. Rather than doing a head count of individual dyslexics, our statistics would show up trends on the basis of which conclusions about dyslexia could be drawn.

Although the number of children tested was 12 905, it was inevitable that in a survey of this magnitude some of the results had to be recorded as 'missing data'. Full details to account for small discrepancies in the number of children tested are given in the original papers. The main thing which we had to be careful about was that there should not be sufficient missing cases to bias our results.

It will be noted, both from this Chapter and from the discussion of the Bangor Dyslexia Test in Chapters 7 and 8, that we specified various different ways of being dyslexic. A child could be dyslexic *either if ... or if ...* Dyslexia, in other words, is a **disjunctive** concept: some limbs of the disjunction need to be present but not all of them and not necessarily the same ones in different individuals. This notion of a disjunctive concept is one to which I shall return in Chapter 23.

NOTES

Note 19.1   The cohort study as a whole was masterminded by Professor Neville Butler, who at the time was Professor of Child Life and Health at Bristol University. Neville has always given me every encouragement, and it was he who first introduced me to Dr Mary Haslum, at the time a research psychologist in his team; my collaboration with Mary has continued to the present day. Later we were joined by Professor T. J. Wheeler, who is a former student of mine and now Vice-Chancellor of the University of Chester. My debt to all of them is immense.

Note 19.2   In 1980 we had, of course, to use the 1979 edition.

Note 19.3   Mary Haslum and I are grateful to Michael Thomson for showing us his research in advance of its publication. The results were later published in Thomson (1982).

Note 19.4   The statistical measures which we used were somewhat complicated; full details will be found in the papers which we published elsewhere (see especially Miles *et al.*, 1998, 2001 and 2003). The scores on the word recognition test were regressed on the combined Similarities–Matrices scores to give for each child an expected reading score. The residual (observed score minus expected score) was then calculated for each child. Those who were between 1 and 1.5 s.d. below prediction were classified as 'moderate underachievers'; those worse than 1.5 s.d. below prediction were classed as 'severe underachievers'. The procedure was repeated in the case of spelling items.

Note 19.5   We know of two such mishaps. In one, an error in the way the word recognition was scored resulted in a slightly enlarged proportion of 'missing data'. Secondly, there were children who failed the Months Forwards test, and in these cases some teachers, quite reasonably, did not proceed to Months Reversed – but a few of them then recorded the result as 'missing data'. We thought it safe in these circumstances to treat an entry of 'missing data' as though it had been a fail. We were prepared to assume that the proportion of 'noise' in the total survey was small enough to be discounted. I do not know if other educational researchers with large data bases experience mishaps of this kind, but I have found none mentioned in the literature.

20 The British Births Cohort Study II

It has been possible up to now to publish seven papers on dyslexia by using data from the British Births Cohort Study. One was a paper written jointly by Mary Haslum and myself (Miles and Haslum, 1986), one a single-authored paper by Mary Haslum (Haslum, 1989) and the remaining five jointly authored by Mary Haslum, Tim Wheeler and myself. Further papers are in preparation.

DYSLEXIA: ANOMALY OR NORMAL VARIATION?

It seemed to us that the first question we should try to answer from the data available from the British Births Cohort Study was whether something called dyslexia really existed. In the 1970s there were many people who asserted that it did not. Before any answer could be attempted, however, it was necessary to specify what exactly the question meant. An important clue to answering the question had been supplied to us by Dr Norman Geschwind (see the recollection at the end of this Chapter). It was obvious that some children had reading and spelling problems, but this did not entail 'the existence of dyslexia' in any worthwhile sense; in the language of Chapter 10, it would not contain any 'bite'.

What we needed to consider was Norman Geschwind's idea of anomaly, as opposed to normal variation. If there was nothing more than normal variation in any of the measures which we judged to be relevant to dyslexia, the scores would conform to the normal (or Gaussian) distribution, which involves plenty of readings at the centre and fewer as you move towards the extremities. If, however, there were significant departures from normality, this would mean that to that extent the anomaly hypothesis had resisted refutation and that there were findings which adherents of the normal variation hypothesis would somehow have to explain away. It was a question, therefore, of finding suitable measures.

In our first analysis we compiled what we called a 'dyslexia index' for all children in the cohort. This involved giving each child 'minus' points if they were above average at reading and at spelling in relation to their intelligence and further 'minus' points if they showed no problems with the supplementary items. If the opposite was the case, 'plus' points were awarded. The 'normal variation' hypothesis predicts that the dyslexia index will be normally distributed.

With scores available for 10992 children the mean for the dyslexia index came out as −0.143, standard deviation (s.d.) 2.995. Table 20.1 shows the distribution.

Table 20.1. Comparison of the two tails of the dyslexia index

	Dyslexia-positive end	Dyslexia-negative end
> 2 < 3 s.d.	410 (3.7%)	63 (0.6%)
> 3 s.d.	67 (0.6%)	0 (0.0%)

Adapted from Miles and Haslum (1986)

It is clear that there were many more scores at the dyslexia-positive end than at the dyslexia-negative end. This result is hard to square with the hypothesis of normal variation.

In a further analysis we checked whether the four supplementary items had any predictive power. If they had not, there would be as many positive indicators among the normal achievers as among the underachievers. Table 20.2 shows the results in the case of both reading and spelling.

Table 20.2. Numbers of positive indicators on the supplementary items (a) for word recognition and (b) for spelling

(a) Word recognition

No. of positive indicators	Underachievers	Overachievers
2	135	38
3	31	5
4	0	1

(b) Spelling

No. of positive indicators	Underachievers	Overachievers
2	127	37
3	26	2
4	0	0

Adapted from Miles and Haslum (1986)

This table shows that among the underachievers there were more positive indicators on the supplementary items than there were among the normal achievers. This result held up both in the case of word recognition and in the case of spelling. This difference would be hard to explain if the four supplementary items were of no value or interest.

We also found that where positive indicators occurred among the overachievers they did so on a random basis, conforming to the Poisson distribution (note 20.1) but not in the case of the underachievers. This provided further confirmation that it was possible to make deductions from the results of the supplementary items which could not otherwise have been made.

The results were compatible with the thesis that dyslexia existed in the sense of being something anomalous and that the supplementary items had a part to play in picking it out.

DYSLEXIA AND THE MIDDLE CLASSES

Next in point of time was the challenge, posed by the notion that, as mentioned in Chapter 12, dyslexia was a middle-class invention: middle-class parents were using this fashionable label as a cover for the fact that their children were not very bright. This was, of course, a sneer and was not intended as a piece of serious research. However, there were already data in the British Births Cohort Study on social class. The children had been classified according to their father's occupation in 1980 into the following groups:

- I and II   Professional occupations
- III nm   Non-manual skilled occupations
- III m   Manual skilled occupations
- IV   Partly skilled occupations
- V   Unskilled occupations

In addition we ourselves had isolated a group which we believed contained a large number of dyslexics and a group of normal achievers for comparison. Data were available on 227 dyslexics and 5959 normal achievers. Table 20.3 shows the number and percentage of dyslexics and controls falling into the six different groups.

Table 20.3. Numbers and percentages of dyslexics and controls in each of the social groups

Social class	Dyslexics		Controls	
	N	%	N	%
I	8	3.52	475	7.49
II	62	27.31	1662	27.89
III nm	22	9.69	601	10.09
III m	97	42.73	2424	40.68
IV	25	11.01	644	10.81
V	13	5.73	153	2.57
TOTAL	227	100	5959	100

Adapted from Miles *et al.* (1994)

When the numbers in groups I, II and III nm were pooled and compared with the pooled numbers in groups III m, IV and V, the difference was non-significant (note 20.2). It is plain from these figures that, whatever reason for the apparent slight excess of dyslexics in group V and the apparent shortfall in group I, the thesis that dyslexia is more common among the middle classes is clearly false.

SHOULD HANDEDNESS BE ROUTINELY RECORDED?

It had been widely supposed over many decades that among dyslexics there was either an excess of left-handers or possibly an excess of those who were neither strongly right-handed nor strongly left-handed. The evidence that this was so was by no means negligible, though my own results had turned out to be negative (Miles, 1993a, Chapter 21). The British Births Cohort Study provided the opportunity for a further check.

Tests of handedness had formed part of a medical examination. Three tests were given: (i) each child was asked to pick up a ball placed 12 inches in front of their feet, (ii) each child was asked to comb their hair and (iii) each child was asked which hand they used for writing. Since the first of these tests was administered twice this gave a total of four tests in all. Five categories of handedness were distinguished:

I. consistent right – those who used their right hand for all four tasks
II. inconsistent right – those who used the right hand for three tasks out of the four
III. ambidextrous – those who used each hand 50% of the time
IV. inconsistent left – those who used the left hand for three tasks out of the four
V. consistent left – those who used the left hand for all four tasks

Full details will be found in the original paper (Miles *et al.* 1996). I present here only the data for the dyslexic group (N = 235) and for the normal achievers (N = 6382). This information is given in Table 20.4.

Table 20.4. Categories of handedness: normal achievers (N = 6382) and dyslexics (N = 235), percentages in brackets

	Normal achievers	Dyslexics
Consistent right	4881 (76.5)	176 (74.9)
Inconsistent right	633 (9.9)	18 (7.7)
Ambidextrous	327 (5.1)	13 (5.5)
Inconsistent left	176 (2.8)	15 (6.4)
Consistent left	365 (5.7)	13 (5.5)

Adapted from Miles *et al.* (1996)

Thus we found no evidence that there was anything unusual about the handedness of dyslexics in comparison with the normal achievers in our study.

Three further papers presenting data from the British Births Cohort Study have been published in *Annals of Dyslexia* (Miles *et al.*, 1998, 2001 and 2003).

GENDER RATIO IN DYSLEXIA

It had been widely supposed from the time of Hinshelwood and Orton that there were more dyslexic males than females. However, quite a stir was created in the 1990s when some researchers in the USA challenged this view (see, in particular, Shaywitz *et al.*, 1990). Head teachers of schools for dyslexic pupils in Britain had always planned for an excess of boys, and if they were now to have an increased intake of girls this would have all kinds of planning implications – more female staff, building of fresh toilets etc.

I looked forward eagerly to reading the paper by Shaywitz *et al.* (1990), but with some scepticism, I must admit. The argument used by Dr Shaywitz and colleagues is an interesting one. They argue that the alleged excess of boys was a consequence of referral bias. This was because boys with educational difficulties were more trouble to teachers than were girls with similar difficulties. The true proportion, they argue, could be determined only by a proper sampling of school populations.

In my own study (Miles, 1993a) there were 182 boys and 41 girls. I therefore had to ask myself if, in accordance with the argument of Shaywitz *et al.*, the excess of males who had come to me for assessment was due to referral bias. These were not children who had been picked out in class because they were a nuisance; they were children who were causing particular concern to their parents because of their literacy problems. Was it conceivable that in these circumstances parents were more than four times as likely to refer their sons rather than their daughters? I did not think so.

I was surprised to find, however, that the definition of dyslexia in the Shaywitz *et al.* paper was simply poor reading in relation to intelligence; there was no reference to poor spelling. They also found, not surprisingly, that children who came out as dyslexic on one occasion and had then improved their reading had thereby ceased to be dyslexic on a later testing. Clearly the authors of the paper were not talking about 'specific developmental dyslexia' in the sense that Dr Macdonald Critchley had promoted, and which was the familiar sense of the word 'dyslexia' in Britain at that time.

When Mary Haslum, Tim Wheeler and I considered how best to present our own data, we thought it tactful to suggest that there could be two different definitions of dyslexia: 'specific reading retardation' (SRR), which our American colleagues had used, and 'specific developmental dyslexia' (SDD), which we ourselves had been using.

In the British Births Cohort Study we found a total of 269 children who satisfied our criteria for being dyslexic – for the most part severe underachievers at spelling who also showed two or more positive indicators on the supplementary items. Of these, 223 were boys and 46 were girls – a ratio of about 4.5:1 (a slight adjustment being made to allow for the greater number of boys overall – 5995 as against 5809 girls). In the case of the 417 severe underachievers who showed few or no indicators of dyslexia there were 243 boys and 174 girls, which gave an adjusted ratio of 1.3:1. Whatever else we had established, it was clear that the four supplementary items were having an effect on the outcome.

There was one particular issue, however, which nearly landed us with a serious problem. We needed to be sure that there was no gender bias in any of the supplementary items. However, we found that many more boys than girls had had difficulty in saying the months of the year correctly. It seemed, therefore, that we had used an item for picking out our dyslexics in which there was an in-built gender bias. However, there was no gender bias in the other three supplementary items, and when the Months Forwards item was omitted the adjusted boy:girl ratio still came out as 4.5:1.

We also decided to check what would happen if we used the same criteria for dyslexia as had our American colleagues. We therefore defined dyslexia as 'poor reading in relation to intelligence' and took the children's results from the Edinburgh Reading Test, which we had not so far used in our other analyses. We obtained a boy: girl ratio of about 1.6:1.

'Poor reading in relation to intelligence' does not seem to me to provide a taxonomy of any strength, whereas what we called in this paper 'SDD', in my view, provides a far more powerful one.

MATHEMATICAL ABILITIES OF 10-YEAR-OLD DYSLEXICS

The next analysis which we carried out was on the mathematics test. To allay possible anxieties on the part of the children the organisers of the Cohort Study designated it 'The Friendly Maths Test'. It comprised 72 items and covered a wide range of mathematical topics, including number, time, length, area, volume, capacity, temperature, mass, money, shape, angles, co-ordinates and statistical tables and graphs. The format was multiple choice. Adjoining each item were five boxes, each with a possible answer, and the children were told to draw a line through the box outside which was the correct answer.

We divided the severe underachievers into the three categories described in the last Chapter – severe underachievers A being those with most indicators of dyslexia, severe underachievers B those with the next most and severe underachievers C those with the fewest. We also wished to compare the scores of the normal achievers. Table 20.5 shows for all four groups the combined score on the Similarities and Matrices tests and the mean scores, with standard deviations, on the Friendly Maths Test.

Table 20.5. Numbers in each group, scores on combined Similarities and Matrices tests and means and standard deviations of their scores on the Friendly Maths test

Group	N	Simil/Mat	Mean score	s.d.
Normal achievers	6338	106.51	49.02	9.56
Moderate underachievers	1703	107.79	47.18	10.72
Severe underachievers C	417	107.97	42.46	10.66
Severe underachievers B	221	106.24	40.95	9.81
Severe underachievers A	269	106.18	39.13	11.96

Adapted from Miles *et al.* (2001)

All four groups were at approximately the same level in respect of their combined scores on the Similarities and Matrices tests; this rules out intelligence level as a possible factor influencing the results. However, severe underachievers A (the dyslexics) obtained significantly lower scores than underachievers C, and even lower scores than either the moderate underachievers or the normal achievers (note 20.3). One must therefore conclude that there are some aspects of mathematics which present dyslexics with distinctive difficulty.

We also found that the dyslexics obtained a lower percentage pass rate on 71 of the 72 items (and in the item which was the exception all groups achieved a pass rate of over 90% correct). On some items, however, the difference in percentage pass rate between dyslexics and normal achievers was only small, whereas on other items this difference was much larger. It was therefore certain particular items which appeared to be presenting the dyslexics with distinctive difficulty, rather than mathematics in general.

As part of the research we asked six panels of judges to discuss among themselves the various items from the Friendly Maths Test and rate on a five-point scale how difficult they thought each item would be for a dyslexic 10-year-old; we found some interesting results. All the judges were experienced teachers of mathematics to dyslexic children, and they made their judgements blind, that is without any knowledge of the figures in our research. There were some items to which the judges unanimously gave a rating of 5 (= very hard for dyslexics) and there were some to which they unanimously gave a rating of 1 (= very easy). For example, two of the items which were adjudged 'very hard' were 432 − 36 and 138 × 7. Among those rated 'very easy' was an item involving counting up 11 stars and a sum involving taking three away from five.

In the great majority of cases the pass rate for underachievers C lay part way between that for the normal achievers and that for underachievers A. This result is compatible with the claim that there are certain things in mathematics which are difficult for dyslexics but not necessarily for severe underachievers who are not dyslexic.

In the light of my own experience and in view of the many insightful comments made by the panels of judges it is perhaps legitimate to speculate as to where their chief difficulties lie. It seems that dyslexics find it hard if they are asked to do calculations where they have to hold in mind a large amount of information at the same time, or if they have to remember complicated algorithms (rules of procedure) and carry out the successive steps in the correct order. In addition their uncertainties over 'left' and 'right' may present them with problems when they are calculating, since with division it is necessary to start on the left, whereas with multiplication, addition and subtraction it is necessary to start on the right. There is no doubt that some dyslexics can be very successful mathematicians (Miles, 2004a). This, I think, is because they can be strong at conceptual thinking, while, after they have reached a certain stage, tiresome problems of calculation can be done by computer.

I shall be considering in Chapter 22 whether there is a syndrome, dyscalculia, separate from the syndrome of dyslexia. What seems clear, both from personal experience and in the light of evidence from the British Births Cohort Study, is that a large number of the mathematical difficulties experienced by dyslexics are part and parcel of their dyslexia.

DYSLEXIA WITHOUT SEVERE LITERACY PROBLEMS

We had already divided the severe underachievers into groups A, B and C according to the extent to which they showed indicators of dyslexia on the supplementary items.

We now decided to extend this A, B and C classification to the cohort as a whole, again excluding the low-ability children. We had already become interested in variants of dyslexia (see Chapter 21), since there seemed to be individuals who showed indicators of dyslexia despite the absence any major literacy problems. As far as the present study was concerned we needed to look among those normal achievers who nevertheless showed significant indicators of dyslexia on the supplementary items.

We therefore made a 3 × 3 table, showing three categories of achievement and three categories of dyslexic indicators. The numbers in each group (with the 'achievement' categories placed horizontally) are set out in Table 20.6.

Table 20.6. Numbers in each group classified in terms of achievement and indicators of dyslexia

Group I 4998	Group II 1159	Group III 417
Group IV 918	Group V 327	Group VI 221
Group VII 422	Group VIII 217	Group IX 269

Low-ability children 3200
Unclassifiable 757[1]
Total 12 905

[1]These were children who could not be assigned to any of the groups because of insufficient data.

Adapted from Miles *et al.* (2003)

It will be seen from this table that there were 422 children in Group VII, that is apparently normal achievers at word recognition and spelling who nevertheless came out with two or more positive indicators of dyslexia or three or more zeros on the supplementary items. At first glance it seemed that these 422 children were cases of false positives – dyslexia-positive according to the supplementary items but falsely so since they appeared to have no literacy problems. If, however, as we now supposed, there could be variants of dyslexia where the literacy problems were minimal, this was the group in which they would be found – seemingly normal achievers who nevertheless seemed to be showing indicators of dyslexia.

The most appropriate comparison group was, of course, Group I – those normal achievers who showed few or no indicators of dyslexia on the supplementary items.

We in fact found that there were available within our data six tests that might be expected to have associations with dyslexia – lower scores on word recognition, spelling, non-word reading, non-word spelling, the Edinburgh Reading Test and the Friendly Maths Test. This number, however, was reduced to five, as we decided not to use the non-word spelling data because there sometimes appeared to be perseveration between the spelling of one non-word and the spelling of the next. This left us with six measures in all, the sixth being gender ratio: if the boy : girl ratio was higher in Group VII than in Group I, this would be evidence that in this group there were more dyslexics.

We therefore compared Groups I and VII in respect of these six criteria. If we were wrong in our hypothesis that some of those in Group VII were dyslexia variants, no differences between Group I and Group VII on any of these measures would be found. Table 20.7 gives the figures. (The term 'residual' indicates a measure of the discrepancy between the observed score and the score predicted on the basis of the subject's intelligence.) Overall, therefore, one would expect the average residual to be somewhere near zero.

Table 20.7. Comparisons between Group I and Group VII

Measure of dyslexia	Group I	Group VII
Word recognition residual	5.38	1.96
Spelling residual	4.74	0.14
Non-word reading	6.62	6.18
Edinburgh Reading	108.07	104.94
Friendly Maths	107.34	102.00
Male : female ratio	43.6% boys	72.3% boys
Total	4998	422

Adapted from Miles *et al.* (2003)

It will be seen that in the case of both word recognition and spelling, Group I were obtaining higher scores in relation to their intelligence than were Group VII. As there were eight non-words to be read, with one point for each one correct, the maximum possible score for non-word reading was eight. With the large numbers of children involved the difference between 6.62 for Group I and 6.18 for Group VII was highly significant. In the case of the Friendly Maths Test it seemed more informative to present standardised scores rather than the raw scores, which we presented in Table 20.5.

Our hypothesis was therefore confirmed: on all six measures Group VII differed from Group I in the expected direction at a high level of confidence (note 20.4).

It seemed to us that the best way of making sense of the results was to suppose that Group VII contained some mild cases of dyslexia – dyslexia variants, if you will – whose literacy problems at age 10 were not a major handicap.

It was these results, too, which led me to question an assumption that I had made from the start of the research – that either you were dyslexic or you were not. It was possible, I supposed, for a person to have a mild form of influenza or to be mildly neurotic; on the other hand it was not possible to be mildly pregnant. I had always assumed that in this respect dyslexia was like pregnancy – either one was dyslexic or one was not, but I now realise that there is a serious possibility that this view may be mistaken.

RECOLLECTIONS

I mentioned in the main text that the inspiration for the Miles and Haslum (1986) paper came from Dr Norman Geschwind. I was lucky enough to be sitting next to him in the coach when those attending an international conference on dyslexia went on a sight-seeing tour in northern Greece, but I fear the sights of northern Greece totally passed me by, so enthralling was Norman Geschwind's conversation. One of the things which he said to me was that he regarded dyslexia as an anomaly. With the impertinence generated as a result of my philosophical training, I asked him what he meant by 'anomaly'. He showed me his hand, pointing out that the fingers of the human hand varied in length – some people's fingers were longer or shorter than those of others. He then said, 'Now imagine a hand with two thumbs – that is what I would call an anomaly.'

This remark made immediate sense to me, and when some years later I was concerned, as I expressed the matter to myself, to 'establish the existence' of dyslexia, I became aware that what needed to be established was the existence of something anomalous – hence the title of our paper (Miles and Haslum, 1986).

NOTES

Note 20.1 In the Poisson distribution, if the overall probability of an occurrence is z, the successive probabilities of none, one, two etc. occurrences is given by the formula:

$$e^{-z}, \quad ze^{-z}, \quad \frac{z^2 e^{-z}}{2!}, \quad \frac{z^3 e^{-z}}{3!}, \text{ etc.}$$

At the dyslexia-negative end there was an almost perfect fit to the Poisson probabilities (chi-squared $= 4.866$, ns. for overachievers at reading and chi-squared $= 3.809$, ns. for overachievers at spelling). In the case of the underachievers there was no fit at all with the Poisson distribution, the chi-squared values being 21.850 ($p < 0.001$) in the case of underachievement at reading and 17.859 ($p < 0.01$) in the case of underachievement at spelling.

Note 20.2 Chi-squared ($df\ 1$) $= 2.37$, ns.

Note 20.3 Analysis of variance revealed absence of homogeneity in the data – $F\ (5,\ 12\,125) = 1249.67$, $p < 0.001$. Post hoc tests (Tukey) showed no significant differences between Group C and Group B and no significant differences between Group A and Group B. All other differences were significant at the level $p < 0.001$.

Note 20.4 For more technical statistical details the reader is referred to the original paper (Miles $et\ al.$, 2003). All six of the comparisons between Group I and Group VII were in the predicted direction at confidence levels of $p < 0.001$.

21 Dyslexia Variants

According to Critchley and Critchley (1978, p 124) there can be dyslexia variants. They write as follows: 'Children are often referred to a doctor on account of a learning disorder or because of inadequacies in written work, where developmental dyslexia seems at first sight not to be the obvious diagnosis if only because the individual's ability to read conforms with both chronological age and intelligence. Might it be that such cases, or at least some of them, can still be looked upon as falling within a rather broader conception of the syndrome of developmental dyslexia? In other words can they be considered as dyslexia variants?'

The Critchleys refer to such cases as 'formes frustes' of dyslexia. According to the dictionary the word 'frustes' has sometimes been used of coins when they are debased in the sense of not being genuine currency. One could perhaps look on the dyslexia variants described in this chapter as 'debased' types of dyslexia – not the classic cases but with the signs present in a less severe form. That there are formes frustes of dyslexia presupposes, of course, that specific dyslexia is an identifiable syndrome; if it were not, this chapter would make no sense.

The idea of variants – cases where one wants to apply the label but where the diagnosis does not fully 'ring true' – are not unknown elsewhere in medicine, for example pigmentation of the arms can be a minor variant in von Recklinghausen disease (note 21.1). In some cases there appears to be a genetic factor at work, with a minor variant of the condition occurring in families where some members are more severely affected.

In what follows I shall present 10 sketches – brief case studies – of individuals whom I suggest should be regarded as dyslexic – but only in an extended sense. I want to say that most of them **were** dyslexic but that, because they need to be included, some widening of the concept of dyslexia is called for. Without such cases the taxonomy provided by the word 'dyslexia' would have been much less strong, whereas the wider concept makes possible the recognition of similarities to the standard cases which would otherwise have been overlooked.

From the late 1960s onwards I had begun to suspect that there were individuals who could be described as 'marginally' dyslexic. There is a chapter with the heading 'Doubtful cases' in Miles (1993b), while in Miles (1993a, p. 52) cases 258 to 264 were showing some signs of dyslexia, but only in a very mild form.

These sketches relate to Fiona, Philip, Mary, Edward, Helen Poole, Rick Loeffler (note 21.2), Charlotte, Professor X, his daughter Joyce and, as a historical reconstruction, the Quaker prison reformer Elizabeth Fry. To preserve anonymity pseudonyms have been used, except, by agreement, in the cases of Helen and Rick.

Philip is described in Chapter 3 (pp. 66–67) of Miles (1993b), while in the same chapter (pp. 69–70) there is an account of Mary and her twin sister Janet. Fiona is case no. 264, p. 52 in Miles (1993a); the brief sketches of Professor X and Joyce have appeared in Miles (2004a, pp. 16–17). Nothing has previously been published on Rick or Charlotte.

SKETCH 1: FIONA

Fiona was assessed by me at the age of nine years three months. On the Schonell R1 test of single-word recognition (Schonell and Schonell, 1952) she had a reading age of 11.0 and on the S1 spelling test a spelling age of 9.2. On selected items of the WISC (Wechsler, 1974) her scaled scores were: Comprehension 20, Similarities 20, Vocabulary 17, Picture Completion 16, Block Design 18 and Object Assembly 14. A score of 16 places a child in the top two and a half per cent of their age group; on any reckoning, therefore, these scores are extremely high. On my method of scoring (see Chapter 9) her results placed her in the Z category, the highest possible and suggestive, at least in some respects, of an IQ in the 140s. When given the Bangor Dyslexia Test, she reported that she had worked out 'left' and 'right' by means of the strategy 'I write with my right hand'. She responded correctly to Months Forwards and Months Reversed, but her mother told me that Fiona had spent considerable time practising them. Her most striking responses, however, occurred when she was asked to repeat three digits in reverse order. In response to 574 she said 'four five seven', and in response to 259 she said 'nine two five'. Spelling errors from her school exercise book included 'siad' for *said*, 'bigst' for *biggest*, 'mosue' for *mouse*, 'chock' for *coach*, 'srroed' for *surrounded*, 'esle' for *else*, 'multplion' for *multiplication*, 'hobing' for *hopping* and 'pruttys' for *prettiest*. Most significantly she had a brother, Terence, who had also been assessed by me and who was severely dyslexic, having literacy problems and a tally of seven and a half positive indicators out of 10 on the Bangor Dyslexia Test. (For more on Terence see Chapter 10.)

SKETCH 2: PHILIP

Philip was referred for assessment at the age of 10 on account of his difficulties with numbers. His headmaster wrote: 'What I find particularly unusual at this age is that he … lacks appreciation of order in numbers. For instance, in simple multiplication involving 3 × 8, he is perfectly liable to put down the 2 in the units column and carry the 4 into the tens column. I have used an abacus and virtually every other method to indicate tens and units to him, but nevertheless mistakes still recur.'

It was found that Philip was of average intelligence and that his reading and spelling ages were within 90% of his chronological age. During the testing he made an error when asked to repeat four digits forwards and another error over three digits reversed – errors which are well outside normal limits for a non-dyslexic 10-year-old of average intelligence. He wrote 'b' in place of 'd' on several occasions, for example he wrote 'boll' for *doll*, 'barsing' for *dancing* and 'binermite' for *dynamite*. He needed to use his fingers for simple calculation; he lost his place in saying his six-times and seven-times tables, and in trying to explain his arithmetical difficulties he said, 'All double numbers – I sometimes put them the wrong way round.' Overall, in what was later to become the Bangor Dyslexia Test, he was found to have five and a half positive indicators. Although he was not seriously retarded in spelling, many of his spelling errors which he made seemed to be of a typically 'dyslexic' kind: 'prepterion' for *preparation* (later 'prparlion'), 'torw brigde' for *Tower Bridge*, 'wroy' for *worry*, 'Amecar' for *America* and 'libtgh' for *light*.

Despite Philip's near-average performance on the reading and spelling tests, there is a dyslexic 'feel' to his case which I do not think can be disputed.

SKETCH 3: MARY

Mary came for assessment at the age of 10. Her twin sister, Janet, had been referred because of suspected dyslexia, and their parents asked whether anyone in the team would like to assess Mary as well even though she was not dyslexic. This offer was accepted.

Both twins turned out to be well above average in intelligence as judged by their results on the WISC-R (Wechsler, 1974). Janet turned out to be dyslexic, as her parents had supposed. In Mary's case, however, as far as her reading and spelling were concerned, there was no trace whatever of dyslexia: on the Schonell tests (Schonell and Schonell, 1952) she had a reading age of exactly 12 years and a spelling age of over 13 years – and this at the age of 10. However, she was found to have four and a half positive indicators on the Bangor Dyslexia Test, with 'pluses' on Left–Right and Digits Forwards and Familial Incidence, as well as 'zeros' on Polysyllables, Tables and Months Reversed – a total of five and a half 'pluses'. The evidence in Miles (1993a, p. 251) suggests that such a high tally of 'pluses', though not unknown, is rare in 10-year-olds who are not dyslexic.

In addition, when Mary was asked to respond to arrays of seven digits which were exposed for eight-tenths of a second, her mean absorption time per array was 3.57 sec. compared with Janet's 4.3 sec. Such data as are available suggest that both these scores are well outside normal limits in respect of time needed for correct responding to arrays of visually presented digits. Inquiries from the family doctor revealed that the twins had separate placentas, thus making it probable that they were dizygotic (non-identical) and therefore different in their genetic make-up.

Before embarking on the present chapter I wrote to both Mary and Janet to ask for their latest news. Both had obtained university degrees and Janet had obtained qualifications at postgraduate level. She says in her letter: 'I am hopeless at proof reading ... I always write down telephone numbers back to front and frequently read out my credit card number wrong ... My spelling is normally the source of much amusement.' Mary writes: 'I have not had any problems with writing or reading ... However, with all my jobs I do find that I have to really concentrate in order to write telephone numbers down correctly. If someone says them quickly, I often get the numbers the wrong way round – that is my only problem really.'

Of all the 10 cases described in this chapter I find Mary the most puzzling – and seemingly the least dyslexic. However, I would suggest with hesitation that the correct description of her is to say that she is a dyslexia variant but that the dyslexia is only very mild.

SKETCH 4: EDWARD

Edward was discovered in 1981 at the age of 14 when control data were being obtained for the Bangor Dyslexia Test. The usual safeguards were specified as to adequate intelligence and opportunity, and in the case of this particular age group it had been decided to accept as controls all those who had spelled 72 or more words correctly on the Schonell S1 spelling test (Schonell and Schonell, 1952). This corresponds to a spelling age of just over 12. (It had been decided that anyone whose spelling was at this level could not be regarded as having any significant dyslexic problems.) Edward spelled 79 words correctly and was therefore included among the controls. Yet his responses on the tables item in the Bangor Dyslexia Test were quite clearly those of a dyslexic: both a medical doctor with considerable experience of dyslexia who was also present and I were agreed on this, and we particularly noticed how other control children at the school could rattle off their tables without the least hesitation.

In view of what I had observed, I spoke to Edward's headmaster, and it was agreed that he should come to Bangor for further assessment. He read 84 out of 100 words correctly on the Schonell word recognition test, which in view of the norms suggested no problems with the reading of single words. However, his mother told me that he had been late in learning to read and still found reading aloud difficult. He was also a slow writer; he had difficulty in learning German words and occasionally read car registration numbers the wrong way round. There was then the chance to give him the Bangor Dyslexia Test in full, not just the seven items used with the control group. His tally of positive indicators came to six: there were 'pluses' on Polysyllables, Tables, Months Reversed, Digits Forwards and Digits Reversed, while there were 'zeros' on the Left–Right and Subtraction items. I found no positive evidence that anyone else in his family was dyslexic.

If one went simply by Edward's reading and spelling scores at the age of 14, there would be no grounds for suspecting dyslexia. However, the cumulative evidence seems to me to leave no doubt that he was dyslexic. If this is right, it is further evidence that cases can be found of individuals who are dyslexic but do not have any significant literacy problems.

SKETCH 5: HELEN

Helen came to see me at the age of 19, kindly offering herself as a 'research case'. At A level she had obtained grade B in both English and French and clearly had no problems with either reading or spelling. However, it became clear that she had had serious problems with calculation.

Her mother wrote: 'Helen was a very active, inquisitive and riotous small child. She talked very early and picked up language easily and quickly.' Tying shoelaces, however, and learning to tell the time were an 'uphill struggle'. Her mother also reported that Helen 'found it impossible to learn times tables. I tried every method possible – chanting, writing down ... large print. Nothing I tried worked and I didn't know why. I could not understand why Helen could not retain this number information in her head as she was a bright child at school [and had] excellent reports for other subjects, especially English, French, etc.'

When I gave Helen the Bangor Dyslexia Test, she showed positive indicators on Left–Right, Tables, Digits Forwards, Digits Reversed and Familial Incidence (her father was reported to be dyslexic) and a zero on Subtraction – the first four sums being answered correctly $(9 - 2, 6 - 3, 19 - 7, 24 - 2)$, but in the case of $52 - 9$ there was a long hesitation before she responded '43' and to arrive at the correct answer to $44 - 7$ she responded, 'Not sure ... $44 - 10$ is 34 ... 37.' Her tally of 'plus' responses on the Bangor Dyslexia Test was thus five and a half.

Here are some extracts from what Helen said in a written account of herself:

> I was often seen as a wilful child who 'closed her mind' to what was being said, and so my 'teachers' [Helen's quote marks] were reluctant to tackle these problems. I began to make my own compensatory strategies to help me work through the problems that I encountered in mathematics ... For all the calculations that I do in my head, I seem to use a 'base' number to work from, like a point of reference ... To overcome the problems I had with fractions I used visual images as reference points, for example birthday cakes with shaded slices or rectangles with shaded slices. This in order to 'see' the $\frac{1}{2}$s and $\frac{1}{4}$s and particularly the more complicated $\frac{3}{4}$s and $\frac{6}{8}$s. (Unfortunately I could not use this method to help me with 'difficult' time signatures which look like fractions and which I could not 'hear' in my head such as 6/8 and 12/8. I could, however, play these signatures if someone was to play music in the signature, so I could get the 'feel' of it to then find my own point of reference from which to remember and work from ... Mathematical exercises which involve a 'mass' of symbols or numbers are, to me, a 'visual nightmare'.

As regards music she writes:

> For me, no one could ever deny the uplifting feeling of an instrument that rested in my hand or lay snugly on my lap ... I can pick up almost any instrument and be playing it within the day whereas I struggle within the 'elementary' system of theory and notation.

This meant that obtaining passes in the various grades of music examination was particularly hard for her. Though she was keen to make a career in music, it is clear that there were certain aspects of music which caused her problems – sight-reading from a score, repeating back a line of melody played on a keyboard, writing out music accurately, transposing music and reading in different clefs.

> I would sit down and try to rote-learn the sequence of letters (note names) that belonged to each key, to apply to the practical performance (I soon forgot them after the performance) … I have found that I do not automatically know what letter or note to associate with the key button or position on the instrument, but I can hear the tone that will come out of the instrument if I press a certain key or move in a certain way … I show only certain 'symptoms' of difficulties encountered by known dyslexic musicians. This may be because I do not suffer from the same disability of letters and words.

SKETCH 6: RICK LOEFFLER

Rick wrote to me from America at the age of 51 on account of his mathematical difficulties. He had read *Dyslexia and Mathematics* (Miles and Miles, 2004), and 'it was like I was reading about myself'. He was interested in moving to a more demanding job but needed a university qualification in mathematics which he had been unable to obtain. He had been told that his disabilities were not of any recognised kind and that he was therefore not eligible for financial help. He told me that he had no reading or spelling problems, and he enclosed a report indicating that he had been found to have a verbal IQ on the WAIS-R (Wechsler, 1992) of 138 and a performance IQ of 111 (full scale IQ = 128).

A copy of the Bangor Dyslexia Test was posted to him so that he could be tested by a qualified psychologist. There were five and a half positive indicators. He reported that his father and brother were dyslexic and that he used to confuse 'b' and 'd'. He told me that in the case of the Left–Right item 'echoing the question helps me to buy time to sort out instructions'. He also indicated that in the Left–Right item he had to imagine himself sitting in the tester's seat. Other comments included: 'I have a hard time remembering instructions partly because of anxiety and the mental gymnastics I must go through to come up with correct answers.' When he attended lectures, he was in difficulty if he tried to listen to the lecture and take notes at the same time.

In a large amount of handwritten correspondence there were almost no spelling errors, though he did at one point write 'rember' for *remember*, and at one point he put 'back wards' in place of *backwards*.

The following are extracts from some of the letters which he sent me by email:

> I have trouble putting things in order quickly, especially when sorting is involved. The symbol >, used in math to indicate greater than or lesser than, is very confusing to me when using the computer. I have trouble with the symbols for up, down and sideways. A strategy is needed for me to distinguish the letters 'b' and 'd'. Proof problems in higher math are frustrating. I can understand the concept being explained only by putting it in my own words – very time consuming! Taking notes I tend to write slowly so I can read what I have written. I have always had difficulty taking notes.

The most significant problem for me is difficulty learning keyboarding and computer operations. It took/takes me longer to learn locations of keys, what the various icons mean, and remembering computer operating instructions. Once learned I do well, but slower. My problems in this area date back to things like learning how to use pocket calculators, operating push button cash registers, etc. My spelling is pretty good but I share Elisabeth Fry's problem (note 21.2) of writing the same words twice (I have to edit whatever I write) be it when using the computer or long hand. I shared Helen's problem of having a hard time learning to tie shoe laces. For the longest time I would tie one-bow. I also share Helen's problems with music notes. To remember a specific note designation and what its placement means is tough ... I scored very high on the Raven Advanced Matrices, but I had to take extra time (on some problems) to make certain I was manipulating the problem correctly. Fortunately, the Raven can be given as an untimed test. My mental processing problems often show up when timed performance is required, thusly creating a problem interpreting test results. On certain timed tests, poor performance can be construed as meaning lack of intelligence or knowledge of the material, but in my situation that is not always true.

Many of Rick's comments seem to me very insightful. It is easy to see how those who control finance need to be sure that financial support goes only to deserving cases, and if an individual does not fit into any recognised category it is easy to assume absence of dessert. It is ironic, however, that Rick would probably have found it easier to obtain support if he had been less intelligent and therefore a worse speller. There are two issues here as far as dyslexia is concerned. Because the phenomena of dyslexia are untidy and involve variants and marginal cases, it does not follow that a given individual has no specific needs. Secondly it is possible that highly intelligent individuals who have worked very hard to overcome their disabilities may thereby disqualify themselves from receiving financial or other help.

Rick also seems to me right about the difficulty in interpreting the results of timed tests in the case of dyslexics: relatively low scores do not necessarily imply lack of intelligence or knowledge but only lack of time.

SKETCH 7: CHARLOTTE

Charlotte wrote to me as follows:

I'm now – at the ripe old age of 60 – reading for a Doctorate in Psychology. I am dreading the time when I have to analyse statistically all the data I have collected on my field-work ... I consistently have a habit of reversing the numbers in my head and writing them down in the wrong order when doing my professional accounts, which drives ... my financial manager to distraction. I am quite incapable of doing mental arithmetic except for overlearned mathematical tables material. The only reason I finally passed General Maths at O level (4th attempt) at the advanced age of 36 prior to going to university to read my first degree was through the understanding of my tutor at the local College of Further Education, who taught me how to translate arithmetical problems into algebraic equations and get the answers that way. I could just about cope with algebra, geometry and trigonometry at O level since I could follow and apply the logic, but sheer computational skills were very difficult. My mind would go blank unless I could visualise simple sums.

As far as language and reading ability is concerned there has never been any problem. I learned to read at the age of 3 and was an avid reader for pleasure as well as school work throughout my career. My spelling is over 95% perfect. I used to have an eidetic memory, which of course has faded quicker than a normal one. I now have to write down every-thing I need to remember ... When under emotional stress or undue pressure of work I get easily disorientated geographically and often lose my way when driving, remembering only the wrong way I went on a previous occasion. When under great stress I can easily confuse 'left' and 'right'. My ability to estimate quantities and sizes is also impaired, and my spatial abilities are not good, nor am I good at judging distances or time.

She concludeds by saying that:

dyscalculia has largely been ignored in comparison (with dyslexia) but the disability can be very demoralising – not to say inconvenient – in this modern world. There must be thousands like me who have struggled with this common condition all their lives.

I was able to give some tests to Charlotte. There were certainly no literacy prob-lems with either reading or spelling: on the Schonell tests (Schonell and Schonell, 1952) she read all the 100 words correctly and made no mistake on the words which had to be spelled – an unusual result as far as I was concerned. I also gave her the Terman–Merrill (1962) vocabulary test, in which the subject is given 45 words to define. The later ones in the list are very obscure and those who define 30 or more of them correctly obtain a pass at the highest grade of 'Superior Adult'. She obtained passes on 42 of them; this is the highest score on the Terman–Merrill Vocabulary test which I have ever encountered.

The results of the Bangor Dyslexia Test were inconclusive. She made one error on the polysyllables item ('an enemy' for *anemone*), made one error over subtrac-tion and, having mistakenly said that eight sevens were 54, she continued by saying that nine sevens were 61. The results on the Left–Right, Months Forwards, Months Reversed, Digits Forwards, Digits Reversed and 'b'–'d' confusion were all negative.

She had, of course, told me in writing that she sometimes confused 'left' and 'right' when under stress, but I am not sure what significance to attach to this. I con-cluded that Charlotte was not dyslexic in the standard sense, but how best to charac-terise calculation problems such as hers will be discussed in the next chapter.

Sketches 8 and 9 are different from the previous seven, since my evidence is second hand. I decided, however, that, despite this and their brevity, they were sufficiently challenging to be worth inclusion. The historical sketch, that of Elizabeth Fry, is different again and exemplifies how dyslexia variants can be of many different kinds.

SKETCH 8: PROFESSOR X

Professor X was a Professor of History with many distinguished publications to his name. He had no difficulties in either reading or spelling. However, he had a real dread of mental arithmetic, which he found extremely difficult. He had some prob-lems with the reading of music, always preferring to play by ear. He failed school certificate mathematics and had to retake the exam. He had difficulty in retaining telephone numbers and even in remembering his own car registration number. He never forgot a person's handwriting. Though forgetful and careless with his own possessions, he always knew where in the house to find a book. He was extremely methodical in making research notes in spite of the appearance of disorder.

SKETCH 9: JOYCE, DAUGHTER OF PROFESSOR X

Joyce was an early reader and never had any difficulty with spelling. However, reading music was always a problem. She was late in learning to tell the time, reading 25 past one as 25 to eleven. Arithmetic became an insurmountable hurdle, and she failed the 11+ exam on account of this but was admitted to the Grammar School at the headmistress's discretion. Mathematics continued to be a nightmare (note 21.3).

SKETCH 10: ELIZABETH FRY

My final sketch is that of Elizabeth Fry, the Quaker prison reformer, who lived from 1780 to 1845. The suggestion that she may have been dyslexic is made by Huntsman and Miles (2002). The main source of evidence is her personal journal, which runs to some 500,000 words and is in her own handwriting (note 21.4). A reproduction of one of the pages is given in Figure 21.1. The date of the entry is 15 July, 1798, when Elizabeth was aged 18.

Some of what Elizabeth Fry wrote is not easy to decipher, but the following appears to be a more or less accurate transcription:

> ... will not always remain equally strong & it does require the strongest resolution always to do right be not the least unkind to any one either behind their ~~faces~~ back or before them do not give way to apetite falcely be chearful & keep most strictly to truth Considering how my day was broken into I spent it well but I fear far from perfect very far I was all the morning imploy'd about the cloths for our journey one thing I feel in the thoughts of it I may see my beloved friend W Savery happy thought but that I leave the rest of the day flew away aunt Gurney was hear we had ...

The three things which one particularly notices in her journals are the frequent spelling errors, the curious handwriting and the almost total absence of punctua-tion. There are many spelling errors in her journals. They include: 'whnet' for *went*, 'impreshon' for *impression*, 'intomit' for *intimate*, 'poeple' for *people* and 'drayhths' for *draughts*.

Critchley and Critchley (1978, pp. 126–7) describe the following variant of dyslexia: 'There is a variant of dyslexia which may present itself in the guise of

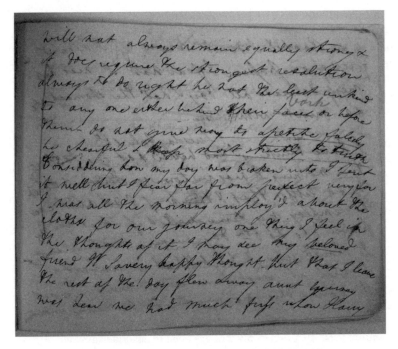

Figure 21.1.   Sample of Elizabeth Fry's handwriting.

atrocious, barely legible handwriting, coupled with a mild degree of spelling disability and unorthodox punctuation.' This description is particularly interesting because of the way in which it fits Elizabeth Fry.

Since the Friends House library also contains letters written by Elizabeth's father and brothers, it seemed worth investigating whether there were signs of dyslexia among members of her family. The result, however, turned out to be negative: there are virtually no spelling errors in any of these letters; the writing is legible and there is no absence of punctuation. However, there is further evidence that Elizabeth Fry was dyslexic, not from her misspellings but from some of the entries in her journals. Small signs may be insignificant on their own but, taken together, can be seen to form a coherent pattern.

She tells us that in 1799 she visited the Quaker school at Ackworth. Here she was asked to test the pupils. After protesting she had only a slight knowledge of grammar, she 'trembled at doing it not a little', when she had to give a report on their 'grammer and syphering' (sic). To add to her embarrassment, 'I was pointedly asked what my opinion was of their spelling.'

At one point she writes in her journal: 'I was thought and called very stupid and obstinate.' She also says: 'I have observed today how slow I am doing things how idly I am inclined – I do things slower than Chenda [her sister Richenda] I see it when we have things to do together'. She also states: 'I cannot help fearing I never shall understand even the common branches of education I have so much slowness in my composition'.

She also had problems of memorising: 'I am so forgetful unless any circumstance particularly impresses', but she does not give specific instances. Elsewhere she writes: 'it seems as if my brain is made of a very soft substance. I receive an idea quickly but it soon vanishes'.

Finally there is evidence of a typically dyslexic error when she repeated some words in a sentence twice over without, apparently, being aware that she had done so. This is the passage:

> I know not what would have been the consiquence (sic) had I had any other than a most careful & wise mother & judicious nurses, if I had been alarmed as too many are by falce (sic) threats of what might happen to me if I did wrong I know not what the consiquence (sic) might have been to me.

OVERALL COMMENTS ON THE SKETCHES

In six cases out of the 10 (Philip, Helen, Rick, Charlotte, Professor X and Joyce) there appeared to be specific problems with calculation. A discussion of whether it is helpful to describe such individuals as 'dyscalculic' will be deferred until the next chapter. In presenting these 10 sketches my aim has been to describe cases which have a dyslexic (or possibly dyscalculic) 'feel' to them even in the absence of any severe literacy problems. In eight of the 10 cases others in the family were affected – the exceptions being Elizabeth Fry and Edward. It seems to me almost certain that in these eight cases a genetic factor was at work. In addition it is clear that in all cases, except possibly that of Mary, there was some kind of 'block' or disability – it was not a question of their 'not being very good at' certain tasks. As in Chapter 20 it is proper to talk of 'anomaly' rather than of 'normal variation'.

If one relied solely on scores on reading and spelling tests, there is a risk that one will fail to detect manifestations which are important and interesting. What is needed, I suggest, is a widening of the concept of dyslexia so that cases such as these can be included.

RECOLLECTIONS

When my son was aged about three, there was an epidemic of mumps in the neighbourhood. It would be incorrect to say that my son caught mumps, but there were miniature swellings round his eyes, with no significant adverse effects on his health. Elaine and I were tempted to call this a case of 'mumplets' rather than of genuine mumps.

When I discovered that Edward (Sketch 4) had such a large number of what seemed like indicators of dyslexia, I was faced with a dilemma – one between common sense and (so it seemed) scientific honesty. The question was whether to retain him among my controls. Common sense suggests that it would be absurd to do so, since there were good reasons to regard him as dyslexic despite his adequate spelling. However, my cut-off point for determining who could count as a control had already been specified, and it was the merest accident that I myself had come on him during the collection of control data, and not one of my colleagues. I decided that, although it might have been more accurate to remove his name, any departure from what I had specified was dishonest. I retained his name, and he appears in Miles (1993a, p. 252) as case no. 111. Fortunately there was enough redundancy in my data to ensure that the conclusions which I drew from my statistics were unaffected.

NOTES

Note 21.1 I am grateful to Professor Neville Butler for supplying me with this example.

Note 21.2 As Rick had expressed an interest I sent him an advance copy of this chapter.

Note 21.3 I am grateful to a third member of this family, herself highly academic and musical, for the information on Professor X and Joyce. I was not able to meet either of them personally: Professor X is no longer alive and Joyce lives many miles away.

Note 21.4 I am grateful to my friend Dr Richard Huntsman for first arousing my interest in the case of Elizabeth Fry. I am also grateful to Joanna Clark, librarian at Friends House, Euston Road, London, for her help in reproducing Elizabeth's own handwriting.

22 Dyslexia and Dyscalculia: Are They Two Separate Syndromes?

The issue of whether there is a separate syndrome, dyscalculia, in addition to the syndrome of dyslexia, is an issue of where to lump and where to split. At present it seems to me that there is insufficient evidence to justify a firm decision in either direction.

I shall assume in what follows that, for reasons set out in Chapter 18, dyslexia is an identifiable syndrome. The question to be discussed is whether the phenomena which constitute what people call 'dyscalculia' can all be explained in terms of a single concept, dyslexia, or whether two separate concepts are needed. According to the principle of Occam's razor, entities (that is concepts) should not be multiplied more than is necessary (note 22.1).

There is no doubt that a large number of the calculation difficulties experienced by dyslexics are part and parcel of their dyslexia. I mentioned in Chapter 20 dyslexics' difficulty in holding in mind a series of mathematical procedures and carrying them out in the right order. There are also the difficulties with subtraction and the recitation of times tables which have been documented in Miles (1993a), and there is now confirmatory evidence (Turner Ellis, 2002) that dyslexic children are slower than controls at carrying out all four of the arithmetical operations – multiplication, division, addition and subtraction. Thus far, nothing beyond the dyslexia concept is needed.

However, it is clear that there are individuals – and one guesses that their numbers are small – who have problems with calculation in the absence of literacy problems. Of the 10 people described in Chapter 21 as manifesting variants of dyslexia, as many as six are possible candidates for inclusion in this group – Philip, Helen, Rick, Charlotte, Professor X and Joyce.

There are, of course, plenty of people who say that they are not very good at mathematics, and it is perhaps useful in this connection to distinguish between a difficulty (not being very good at something) and a deficit or disability. Two criteria suggest themselves for deficit or disability – resistance to standard teaching methods and the presence of a similar problem in one or more members of the same family. Disabilities can sometimes be compensated for by the use of alternative strategies – Charlotte's ability to do mathematical calculations when she was shown how to do them by algebra appears to be a case in point – but it is typical of a disability that it evokes the comment, 'We tried everything.'

In these six cases it seems clear that what was involved was a deficit or disability. Arguably, however, there is enough evidence in the cases of Philip, Helen and Rick to suggest that the problems belonged in the dyslexia family rather than requiring a new concept, that is dyscalculia. Philip's spelling was bizarre, to say the least, and he confused 'b' and 'd'; both Helen and Rick were extremely bright, which may have made spelling less of a problem, and it is surely significant that both had dyslexic fathers.

This leaves Charlotte, Professor X and Joyce, none of whom had any literacy problems. If the word 'dyscalculia' is to be used at all, it seems appropriate that it should be used only of those who have calculation problems in the absence of literacy problems.

Charlotte replied 'an enemy' in place of *anemone* on the Bangor Dyslexia Test, and it is possible that Professor X and Joyce had significant difficulties in reading musical notation. These, however, are the flimsiest possible grounds for saying that they were dyslexic. Might one therefore argue that these three individuals, and anyone like them, should be described not as dyslexic but as dyscalculic?

There is a complication in that the word 'dyscalculia' has been used by Butterworth (1999) to refer to what he regards as a highly specific calculation difficulty. A brief discussion of some of Butterworth's ideas, including a reference to his *Dyscalculia Screener* (Butterworth, 2003) will be found in Miles (2004a). One of my worries about this 'Screener' test is that it seems to me it will probably pick up a number of dyslexics, in my sense of the word – those who have literacy problems as well as calculation problems. Pending further research it seems to me wise to keep an open mind as to what will be the future of the concept of dyscalculia in Butterworth's sense.

In the meantime I offer the following speculations on the theoretical side. For any child at a very young age a heard sound is just a noise – that and no more. Soon, however, the child is able to appreciate that heard sounds **stand for** something, and in due course the child learns to talk and, later, all being well, to read.

For the non-dyslexic child physical stimuli (energy changes in the environment) can be converted into symbols during the normal course of development. For the dyslexic child, however, the ability to recognise symbols does not come easily and takes longer to become automatic. This suggestion is, of course, in line with that made by Nicolson and Fawcett (1990), who suggest that slowness in acquiring automaticity is a central feature in dyslexia. Once they have learned the meaning of a particular symbol, dyslexics' reasoning powers are on a level with those of their non-dyslexic peers; this is why on the reasoning items which occur in traditional intelligence tests they tend to score highly.

Now it would seem that in some cases the deficit is restricted to symbols for number. If we are to use the word 'dyscalculic', it makes sense to use it to refer only to those individuals for whom number symbols rather than symbols for sounds (that is letters of the alphabet) present difficulty.

If one then asks why the ability to symbolise numbers should sometimes be selectively impaired, the answer must presumably lie in the very abstract nature of numbers. If a link is learned between the heard sound 'four' and the written mark '4' (what we call the arabic numeral), there needs to be yet a further 'paired association' between the auditory and visual stimuli and the concept of four objects. Ability to read presupposes the ability to treat letters and sounds as equivalent; ability to calculate presupposes something superimposed on this – not just a letter–sound correspondence or numeral–sound correspondence (hard as these are for dyslexics to achieve), but the appreciation of a further set of equivalence relations – those between sounds, numerals and a specific number of objects.

Calculation, then, may be selectively impaired. What this involves can be regarded as a kind of second-order failure – not just between the ability to associate letters of the alphabet or numerals with their names but the ability to associate the numeral and its name with events in the world, for example four apples or six bananas.

How, then, do we classify this kind of selective impairment? It is possible, I think, to regard it as an extra complication superimposed on the person's dyslexia rather than as a separate syndrome. All this, however, is extremely speculative, and it may well be that new discoveries – perhaps involving those who lack any basic sense of number – may dispose us to lump and split in different ways. It seems to me that at present the matter remains open.

NOTE

Note 22.1   For those who prefer the Latin version it is: *entia non sunt multiplicanda praeter necessitatem*. There is, however, a counter principle which is sometimes overlooked: *entium varietates non temere sunt minuendae* – which means, approximately: 'Do not use fewer concepts when you need more.' See, in this connection, Kant (1781).

23 Dyslexia as a Disjunctive Concept

I suggested, particularly in Chapters 7 and 8 and in Chapters 19 and 20, that dyslexia is a disjunctive concept. This means that there are different ways of being dyslexic: in one person it may be manifestations A, B, F and G; in another person it may be manifestations B, C, D and H, and so on. No one manifestation is crucial; what is crucial is the way in which the manifestations combine. According to the arguments in this book it is possible to be dyslexic without necessarily being a poor reader, that is to say poor reading is not a necessary condition for being dyslexic. It is also possible to be a poor reader without being dyslexic, which is the same as saying that neither is poor reading a sufficient condition for being dyslexic.

I want to argue in this chapter that the word 'dyslexia' is also what Ryle (1949) would have called a 'disposition' word. What he had in mind can best be shown by means of examples. It was characteristic of Ryle to draw on the familiar events of ordinary life and use them to illustrate important philosophical insights.

If we describe a person as 'bad tempered', this does not imply that that person is actually doing anything here and now; it is a statement about tendencies – about how the person tends to behave in particular circumstances. Thus a bad-tempered person might respond irritably when there was no provocation, or for no particular reason might kick the cat.

At this point I should like to re-introduce some technical terms which I first used many years ago. In a paper entitled 'On defining intelligence' (Miles, 1957) I argue that, like 'bad tempered', 'intelligence' is a disposition word. I then add two further technical terms: I refer to the word 'intelligence' as the **substrate** and to the ways in which intelligence manifested itself as the **exemplaries**. Thus 'bad tempered' would be the substrate, while flying into an unprovoked rage, kicking the cat etc. would be the exemplaries.

It will be noted that in this case, as in many others, the list of exemplaries is open-ended and indefinite – there are many different ways in which one can display bad temper. Also there may be circumstances in which the same physical movements involved in kicking the cat may not be an expression of bad temper, but, for instance, a necessary step in preventing the cat from getting at the cream.

In a posthumously published paper Ryle (2000) shows how some behavioural manifestations can be part of a **course of action**. Thus one such course of action might be to train a puppy. This can be done by stroking it, whistling to it, giving it a piece of meat when it comes in response to a whistle etc. All this is carried out in a systematic way over a period of time. The trainer, however, may sometimes whistle out of *joie de vivre* or stroke the puppy when this is not part of a course of training. Ryle's point is that what is physically the same behaviour may occur in many different contexts, and it is the context in which it occurs that gives the behaviour its significance.

Now although with most disposition words the list of exemplars is open-ended, it is possible, if one so wishes, to make them detailed and specific. This is what has happened in the case of intelligence. If we go by what people say when they are not using psychological technical terms, there are many different ways in which one can show oneself to be intelligent. However, as I point out (Miles, 1957), psychologists have **operationalised** the concept of intelligence – they have specified, with a large amount of detail, what should count as exemplars of the word 'intelligent', namely particular responses to items in the Terman–Merrill, Wechsler and other intelligence tests. Some people at the time thought that the dictum 'intelligence is what intelligence tests measure' was circular and therefore uninformative. The dictum, however, can be seen as a way of indicating that the substrate 'intelligent' should be defined in terms of its exemplars.

In another publication (Miles, 1966, Chapter 10) I thought it would be helpful to distinguish between 'greater' and 'lesser' exemplars. Greater exemplars are those which involve typical or standard cases of the behaviour in question. Thus an arrival on time would be a greater exemplary of the substrate 'punctual' – it is a sample of punctuality, and a series of regular arrivals on time would make it true by definition that the person was punctual. In contrast, if someone ran for cover on several occasions, this would be a lesser exemplary of the substrate 'easily scared', since one could not be sure that the description 'easily scared' was appropriate if one did not know in what context the runnings for cover took place.

* * *

How, then, are all these considerations relevant to dyslexia? My thesis is that the word 'dyslexia' is similar to the disposition words whose logical behaviour has been described by Ryle (1949). Because dyslexia is a disjunctive concept, it has many different exemplars – there are many different ways of showing that one is dyslexic. Examples of its exemplars will be found in the Bangor Dyslexia Test (Miles, 1997), as well as in some of the many different tests of phonological awareness now in common use, for example Frederickson et al. (1997). For a person to be dyslexic it is necessary for there to be a sufficient number of exemplars, but there is no need to specify a precise number; the questioin is rather, 'Are these seeming exemplars fortuitous and therefore insignificant or are there enough of them to make it likely that further exemplars will be forthcoming?'

In the Bangor Dyslexia Test there is even a built-in procedure for distinguishing greater from lesser exemplars: the lesser exemplars are responses which are scored as 'zero', for instance echoing the question or requesting that it be repeated.

To say 'This person is dyslexic' is, in effect, to make a bet that further manifestations of dyslexia will occur in the future; if the diagnosis is wrong, no such manifestations will be forthcoming. The thesis of this book is that these manifestations, taken in conjunction, constitute a powerful taxonomy.

References

Augur, J. and Briggs, S. (1992) *The Hickey Multisensory Language Course*, Whurr, London.

Baddeley, A.D., Ellis, N.C., Miles, T.R. and Lewis, V. (1982) Developmental and acquired dyslexia: a comparison. *Cognition*, 11 (2), 185–199.

Black, S.R. (2001) Semantic satiation and lexical resolution. *American Journal of Psychology*, 114 (4), 493–510.

Blanchard, P. (1946) Psychoanalytic contributions to the problems of reading disabilities. *Psychoanalytic Study of the Child*, 2, 163–187. See in particular Case 3, especially pp. 175 and 182.

Bullock Report (1975) *A Language for Life*, HMSO, London.

Burt, C. (1947) *Mental and Scholastic Tests*, Staples, London.

Butterworth, B. (1999) *The Mathematical Brain*, Macmillan, London.

Butterworth, B. (2003) *Dyscalculia Screener*, NFER-Nelson, Windsor.

Cooke, E.A. (1993) *Tackling Dyslexia the Bangor Way*, Whurr, London.

Cooke, E.A. (2002) *Tackling Dyslexia*, Whurr, London.

Critchley, M. (1970) *The Dyslexic Child*, Heinemann, London.

Critchley, M. (ed) (1978) *Butterworth's Medical Dictionary*, Butterworths, London.

Critchley, M. and Critchley, E.A. (1978) *Dyslexia Defined*, Heinemann, London.

Davis, D.R. and Cashdan, A. (1963) Specific dyslexia. *British Journal of Educational Psychology*, 33 (1), 80–82.

Denckla, M.B. and Rudel, R.G. (1976) Naming of object drawings by dyslexic and other learning disabled children. *Brain and Language*, 3, 1–15.

Done, D.J. and Miles, T.R. (1988) Age of word aquisition in developmental dyslexics as determined by response latencies in a picture naming task, in *Practical Aspects of Memory: Current Research and Issues,* vol. 2, (eds M.M. Gruneberg, P.E. Morris and R.N. Sykes), John Wiley & Sons, Ltd, Chichester.

Edinburgh Reading Test (1985) Hodder and Stoughton, London.

Elliott, C.D., Murray, D.J. and Pearson, L.S. (1983) *The British Ability Scales*, NFER-Nelson, Windsor.

Ellis, N.C. and Miles, T.R. (1977) Dyslexia as a limitation in the ability to process information. *Bulletin of the Orton Society* (now *Annals of Dyslexia*), 27, 72–81.

Ellis, N.C. and Miles, T.R. (1978) Visual information processing in dyslexic children, in *Practical Aspects of Memory*, (eds M.M. Gruneberg, P.E. Morris and R.N. Sykes), Academic Press, London.

Frederickson, N., Frith, U. and Reason, R. (1997) *The Phonological Assessment Battery (PhAB)*, NFER-Nelson, Windsor.

Ganschow, L., Lloyd Jones, J. and Miles, T.R. (1994) Dyslexia and musical notation. *Annals of Dyslexia*, 44, 185–201.

Gillingham, A. and Stillman, B.E. (1956) *Remedial Training for Children with Specific Difficulty in Reading, Spelling and Penmanship*, Educators' Publishing Service, Cambridge, MA.

Goodman, K. (1967) Reading: a psycholinguistic guessing game. *Journal of the Reading Specialist*, 6 (1), 126–135.

Hales, G. (ed) (1994) *Dyslexia Matters: A Celebratory Contributed Volume to Honour Professor Miles*, Whurr, London.

Hallgren, B. (1950) Specific Dyslexia (Congenital Word-Blindness): a clinical and genetic study. *Acta Psychologica et Neurologica, Supplementum* 65: i–xi and 1–287.

Hampshire, S. (1981) *Susan's Story*, Sidgwick and Jackson, London.

Hansard (1987) House of Commons debate, 13 July 1987, col. 950, HMSO, London.

Harzem, P. and Miles, T.R. (1978) *Conceptual Issues in Operant Psychology*, John Wiley & Sons, Ltd, Chichester.

Haslum, M.N. (1989) Predictors of dyslexia? *Irish Journal of Psychology*, 10 (4), 622–630.

Haslum, M.N. and Miles, T.R. (in press) Motor performance and dyslexia in a national cohort of 10-year-old children. *Dyslexia: An International Journal of Research and Practice*.

Head, H. (1926) *Aphasia and Kindred Disorders of Speech*, Macmillan, London.

Henderson, A. and Miles, E. (2001) *Basic Topics in Mathematics for Dyslexics*, Whurr, London.

Hermann, K. (1959) *Reading Disability: A Medical Study of Word-Blindness and Related Handicaps*, Munksgaard, Copenhagen.

Hinshelwood, J. (1917) *Congenital Word-Blindness*, H.K. Lewis, London.

Hornsby, B. (1989) *Before Alpha*. Souvenir Press, London.

Hornsby, B. and Miles, T.R. (1980) The effects of dyslexia-centred teaching. *British Journal of Educational Psychology*, 50, 236–242.

Hornsby, B. and Shear, F. (1975) *Alpha to Omega*, Heinemann, London.

Huntsman, R.G. and Miles, T.R. (2002) The stupidity of Elizabeth Fry: was it dyslexia? *British Journal of General Practice* (December), 1042–1043.

Kant, I. (1781) *Critique of Pure Reason*, (tr. N. Kemp Smith), Macmillan, London, 1929.

Kershaw Report (1974) People with Dysleixa: Report of a working party commissioned by the British Council for the rehabilitation of the disabled, British Council for the Rehabilitation of the Disabled, London.

Kibel, M. (2004) *Phonetic accuracy in the spelling of dyslexic and normally achieving children: similarities and differences*. University of Liverpool. Ph.D. thesis.

Kibel, M. and Miles, T.R. (1994) Phonological errors in the spelling of taught dyslexic children, in *Reading Development and Dyslexia*, (eds C. Hulme and M. Snowling), Whurr, London, pp. 105–127.

Klopfer, B. and Kelley, D.M. (1943) *The Rorschach Technique*, World Book Co, New York.

Koffka, K. (1935) *Principles of Gestalt Psychology*, Harcourt Brace, New York.

Konigsberg, R. (ed) (1989) *Churchill's Medical Dictionary*, Churchill Livingstone, New York.

Kounios, J., Katz, S.A. and Holcomb, P.J. (2000) On the locus of the semantic satiation effect: evidence from brain potentials. *Memory and Cognition*, 26 (8), 1366–1377.

Macmeeken, M. (1939) *Ocular Dominance in Relation to Developmental Aphasia*, University of London Press.

Miles, E. (2000) Dyslexia may show a different face in different languages. *Dyslexia: An International Journal of Research and Practice*, 6 (3), 193–207.

Miles, E. and Miles, T.R. (1994) The interface between research and remediation, in *Handbook of Spelling: Theory, Process and Intervention*, (eds G.D.A. Brown and N.C. Ellis), John Wiley & Sons, Ltd, Chichester, pp. 441–458.

Miles, T.R. (1957) On defining intelligence. *British Journal of Educational Psychology*, 27 (3), 153–165.

Miles, T.R. (1959) *Religion and the Scientific Outlook*, Allen and Unwin, London.

Miles, T.R. (1961) Two cases of developmental aphasia. *Journal of Child Psychology and Psychiatry*, 1 (2), 48–70.

Miles, T.R. (1962) A suggested method of treatment for specific dyslexia, in *Word-Blindness or Specific Developmental Dyslexia*, (ed A. White Franklin), Proceedings of a conference called by the Invalid Children's Aid Association 12 April 1962, pp. 99–104.

Miles, T.R. (1966) *Eliminating the Unconscious: A Behaviourist Approach to Psychoanalysis*, Pergamon Press, Oxford.

Miles, T.R. (1967) In defence of the concept of dyslexia, in *The Second International Reading Symposium* (eds J. Downing and A.L. Brown), Cassell, London, pp. 242–260.

Miles, T.R. (1970) *On Helping the Dyslexic Child*, Methuen, London.

Miles, T.R. (1971) More on dyslexia, *British Journal of Educational Psychology*, 41 (1), 1–5.

Miles, T.R. (1976) The Jensen debate. *Philosophy*, 51, 196.

Miles, T.R. (1986) On the persistence of dyslexic difficulties into adulthood, in *Dyslexia: Its Neuropsychology and Treatment*, (eds G.T. Pavlidis and D.F. Fisher), John Wiley & Sons, Ltd, Chichester, pp. 149–163.

Miles, T.R. (1988) Counselling in dyslexia. *Counselling Psychology Quarterly*, 1 (1), 97–107.

Miles, T.R. (1993a) *Dyslexia: The Pattern of Difficulties*, (2nd edn), Whurr, London.

Miles, T.R. (1993b) *Understanding Dyslexia*, Amethyst Books, Bath.

Miles, T.R. (1994) A proposed taxonomy and some consequences, in *Dyslexia in Children: Multidisciplinary Perspectives*, (eds A.J. Fawcett and R.I. Nicolson), Harvester Wheatsheaf, London, pp. 195–214.

Miles, T.R. (1996) Do dyslexic children have IQs? *Dyslexia: An International Journal of Research and Practice*, 2 (3), 175–178.

Miles, T.R. (1997) *The Bangor Dyslexia Test*, Learning Development Aids, Wisbech, Cambridge.

Miles, T.R. (1998) *Speaking of God: Theism, Atheism and the Magnus Image*, Sessions, York.

Miles, T.R. (2004a) The nature of dyslexia, in *Dyslexia and Mathematics*, (eds T.R. Miles and E. Miles), RoutledgeFarmer, London.

Miles, T.R. (2004b) Fifty years of dyslexia research: a personal story. *Dyslexia Review*, 16 (1), 4–7.

Miles, T.R. and Miles, E. (1975) *More Help for Dyslexic Children*, Methuen Educational, London.

Miles, T.R. and Wheeler, T.J. (1977) Responses of dyslexic and non-dyslexic subjects to tachistoscopically presented digits. *IRCS Medical Science, Psychology and Psychiatry*, 5, 149.

Miles, T.R. and Ellis, N.C. (1981) A lexical encoding difficulty II, in *Dyslexia Research and Its Applications to Education* (eds T.R. Miles and G.T. Pavlidis), John Wiley & Sons, Ltd, Chichester.

Miles, T.R. and Miles, E. (1983a) *Help for Dyslexic Children*, Routledge, London.

Miles, T.R. and Miles, E. (1983b) *The Teaching Needs of 7-year-old Dyslexic Children*. Report submitted to the Department of Education and Science, HMSO, London.

Miles, T.R. and Haslum, M.N. (1986) Dyslexia: anomaly or normal variation? *Annals of Dyslexia*, 36, 103–117.

Miles, T.R., Wheeler, T.J. and Haslum, M.N. (1994) Dyslexia and the middle classes. *Links 2*, 1 (2), 17–19.

Miles, T.R., Haslum, M.N. and Wheeler, T.J. (1996) Handedness in dyslexia: should this be routinely recorded? *Dyslexia Review*, 8 (2), autumn, 7–9.

Miles, T.R., Haslum, M.N. and Wheeler, T.J. (1998) Gender ratio in dyslexia. *Annals of Dyslexia*, 48, 27–55.

Miles, T.R. and Miles, E. (1999a) *Dyslexia: A Hundred Years On*, Open University Press, Ballmoor, Bucks.

Miles, T.R. and Miles, E. (1999b) Dyslexia, in *Dyslexia, Autism, Mental Retardation*, (eds D. Wimpory, S. Nash, and N. Kurian), Grace Academic Publications, Kerala, India.

Miles, T.R., Haslum, M.N. and Wheeler, T.J. (2001) Mathematical abilities of 10-year-old dyslexic children. *Annals of Dyslexia*, 51, 299–321.

Miles, T.R. and Gibbons, S.L. (2002) Colour naming in dyslexic and non-dyslexic adults. *Dyslexia Review*, 13 (2), 4–6.

Miles, T.R., Wheeler, T.J. and Haslum, M.N. (2003) Dyslexia without severe literacy problems. *Annals of Dyslexia*, 53, 340–350.

Miles, T.R. and Miles, E. (eds) (2004) *Dyslexia and Mathematics*, RoutledgeFalmer, London.

Miles, T.R., Thierry, G., Roberts, J. and Schiffeldrin, J. (in press) Verbatim and gist recall of sentences by dyslexic adults. *Dyslexia: An International Journal of Research and Practice*.

Miller, G.A. (1966) *Psychology: The Science of Mental Life*, Pelican, Harmondsworth.

Morgan, W.P. (1896) A case study of congenital word-blindness. *British Medical Journal*, 2, 1378.

Naidoo, S. (1972) *Specific Dyslexia*, Pitman, London.

Nicolson, R.I. and Fawcett, A.J. (1990) Automaticity: a new framework for dyslexia research. *Cognition*, 35, 158–182.

Nicolson, R.I. and Fawcett, A.J. (1995) Dyslexia is more than a phonological difficulty. *Dyslexia: An International Journal of Research and Practice*, 1 (1), 19–36.

Orton, S.T. (1937) *Reading, Writing and Speech Problems in Children*, Chapman & Hall, London.

Orton, S.T. (1989) *Reading, Writing and Speech Problems in Children and Selected Papers*, Pro-Ed, Austin, TX.

Poole, H. (2001) My music and my dyscalculia, in *Music and Dyslexia: Opening New Doors*, (eds T.R. Miles and J. Westcombe), Whurr, London, pp. 53–56.

Popper, K.R. (1963) *Conjectures and Refutations*, Routledge and Kegan Paul, London.

Ramaa, S., Miles, T.R. and Lalithamma, M.S. (1993) Dyslexia: symbol processing in the Kannada language. *Reading and Writing*, 5 (1), 29–41.

Raven, J.C. (1965) *Advanced Progressive Matrices*, H.K. Lewis, London.

Rook, K. and Miles, T.R. (1999) Can dyslexics succeed at university? *Dyslexia Review*, 11 (2), 8–11.

Ryle, G. (1949) *The Concept of Mind*, Hutchinson, London.

Ryle, G. (2000) Course of action. *Philosophy*, 75 (3), 331–344.

Schonell, F.J. (1945) *The Psychology and Teaching of Reading*, Oliver & Boyd, Edinburgh.

Schonell, F.J. and Schonell F.E. (1952) *Mental and Scholastic Tests*, Oliver & Boyd, Edinburgh.

Shaywitz, S.E., Shaywitz, B.A., Fletcher, J.M. and Escobar, M.D. (1990) Prevalence of reading disability in boys and girls. *Journal of the American Medical Association*, 264 (3), 998–1002.

Sidgwick, H. (1922) *Methods of Ethics*, Macmillan, London.

Spearman, C. (1927) *The Abilities of Man*, Macmillan, New York.

Stirling, E.G. and Miles, T.R. (1988) Naming ability and oral fluency in dyslexic adolescents. *Annals of Dyslexia*, 38, 50–72.

Terman L.M. and Merrill, M.A. (1937, 1960) *Measuring Intelligence*, Harrap, London.

Thomson, M.E. (1982) The assessment of children with specific reading difficulties (dyslexia) using the British Ability Scales. *British Journal of Psychology*, 73 (4), 461–478.

Tizard Report (1972) *Children with Specific Reading Difficulties*. Report of the Advisory Committee on Handicapped Children, HMSO, London.

Turner Ellis, S.A. (2002) *Correctness and Speed of Dyslexics and Non-Dyslexics on the Four Mathematical Operations*. University of Liverpool. Ph.D. thesis.

Turner Ellis, S.A., Miles, T.R. and Wheeler, T.J. (in preparation) Extraneous behaviour on the part of dyslexic children during the carrying out of computational tasks.

Warnock Report (1978) *Special Educational Needs*. Report of the Committee of Enquiry into the Education of Handicapped Children and Young People, HMSO, London.

Wechsler, D. (1949) *Wechsler Intelligence Scale for Children* (WISC), The Psychological Corporation, New York.

Wechsler, D. (1974) *Wechsler Intelligence Scale for Children – Revised*, The Psychological Corporation, New York.

Wechsler, D. (1992) *Wechsler Adult Intelligence Scale – Revised*, The Psychological Corporation, New York.

White Franklin, A. (ed) (1962) *Word-Blindness or Specific Developmental Dyslexia*. Proceedings of a conference called by the Invalid Children's Aid Association, Pitman, London.

Wickson, T.J. (1993) *Dyslexia and Bizarre Spellings*, University of Wales, Bangor. M.Ed. dissertation.

Williams, A.L. and Miles, T.R. (1985) Rorschach responses of dyslexic children. *Annals of Dyslexia*, 35, 51–66.

Index

(Note. Where tests taken from the Wechsler Intelligence Scale for Children, the British Ability Scales and the Bangor Dyslexia Test are mentioned they have been abbreviated, respectively, to WISC, BAS and BDT).